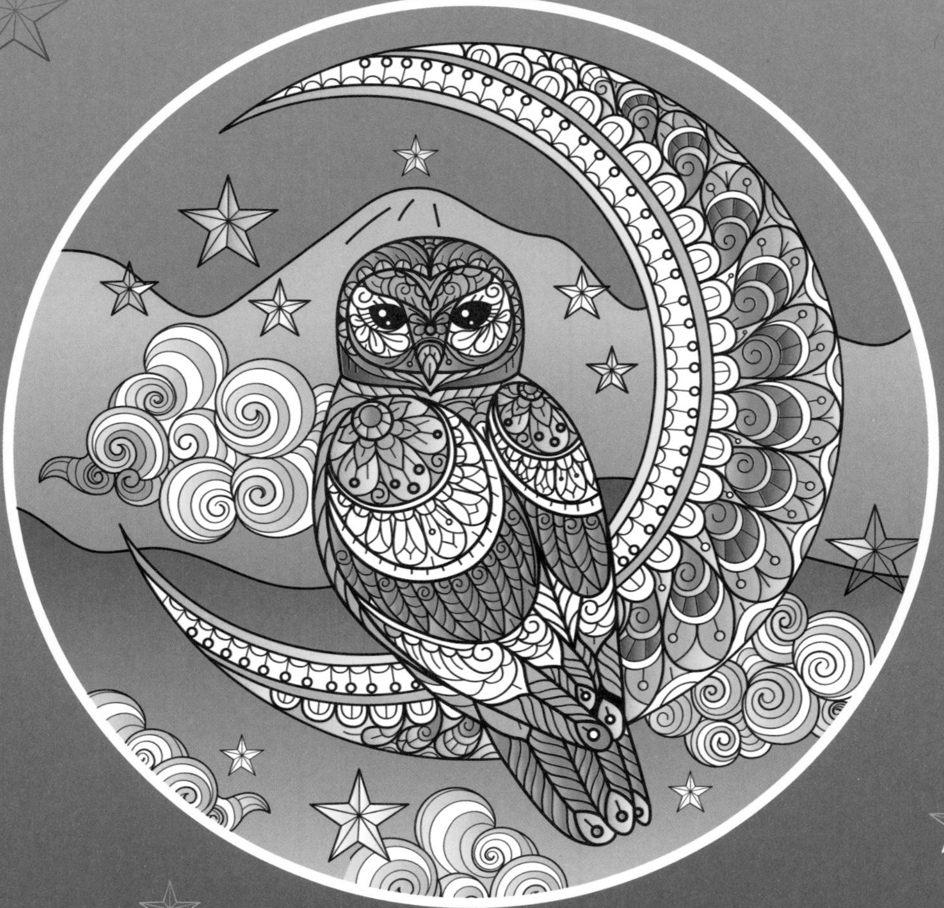

CELESTIAL MAGIC

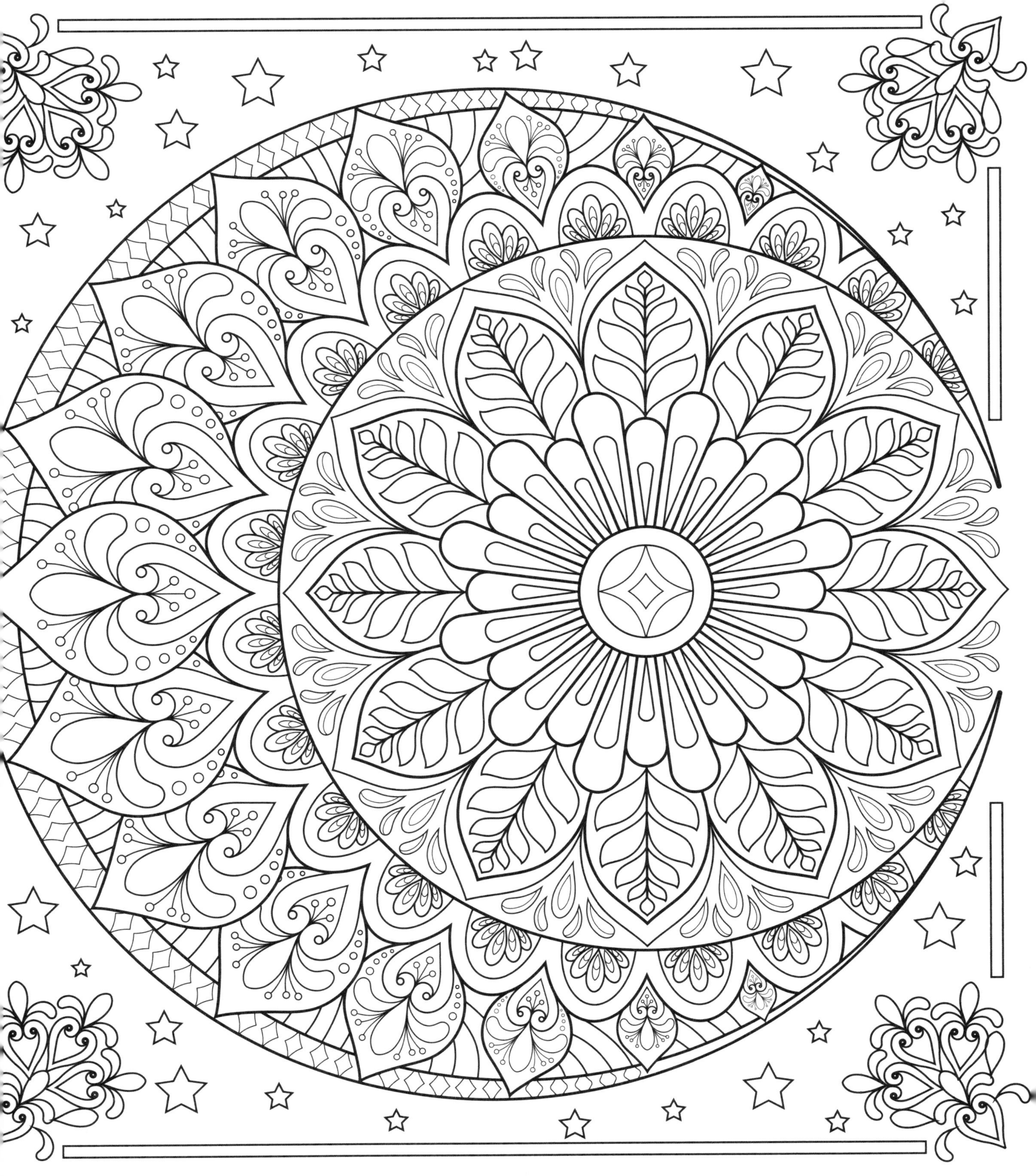

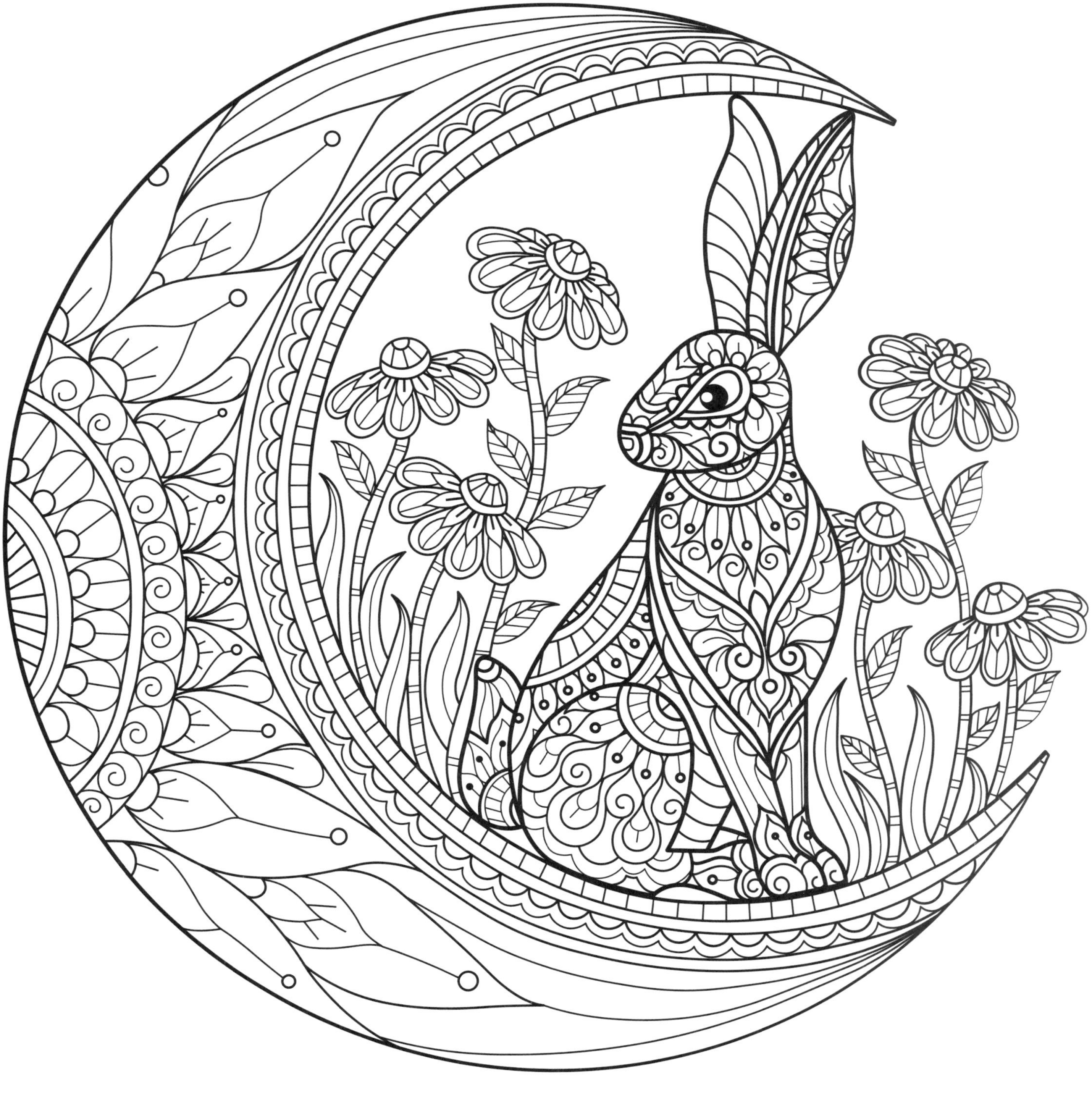

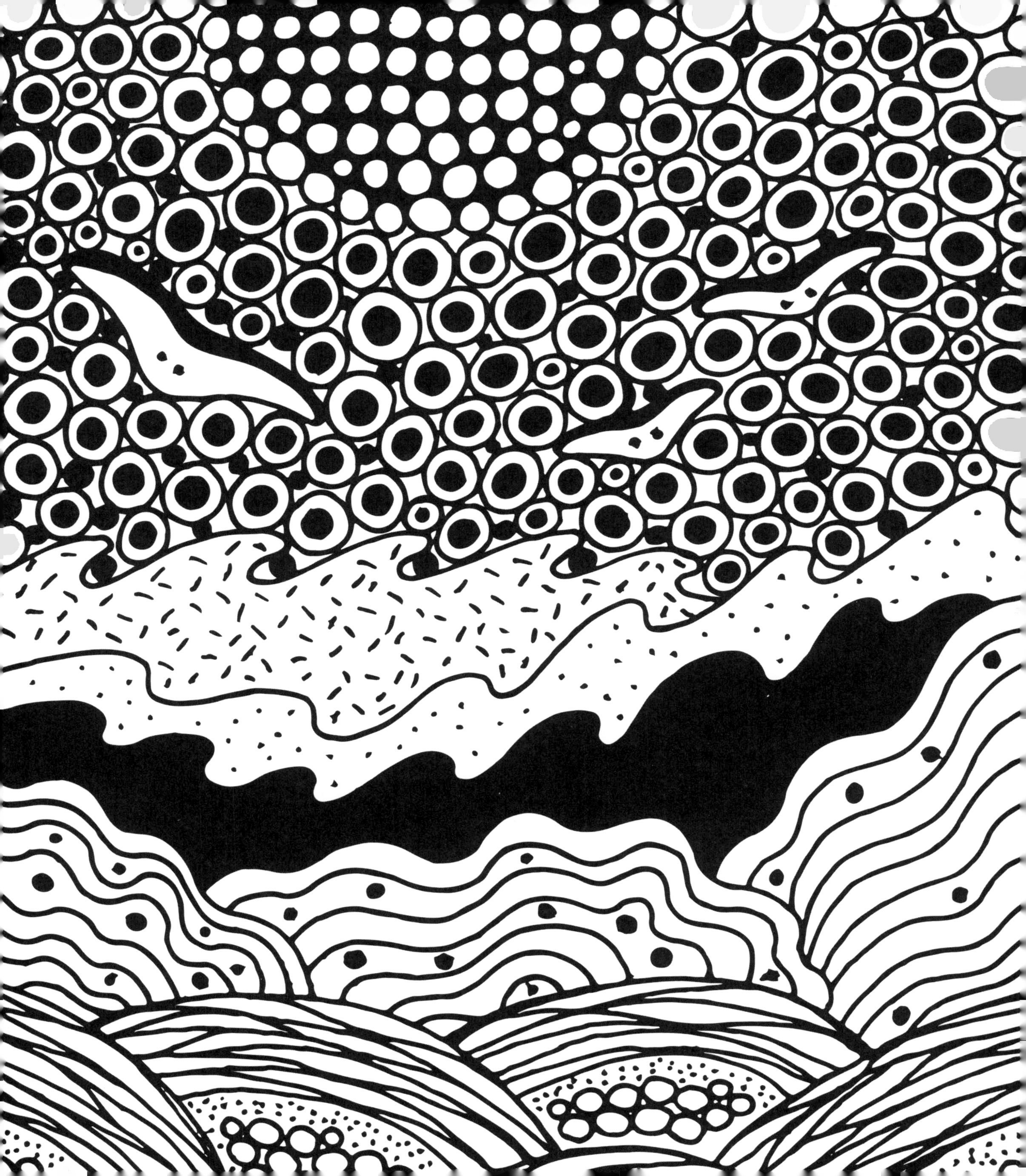

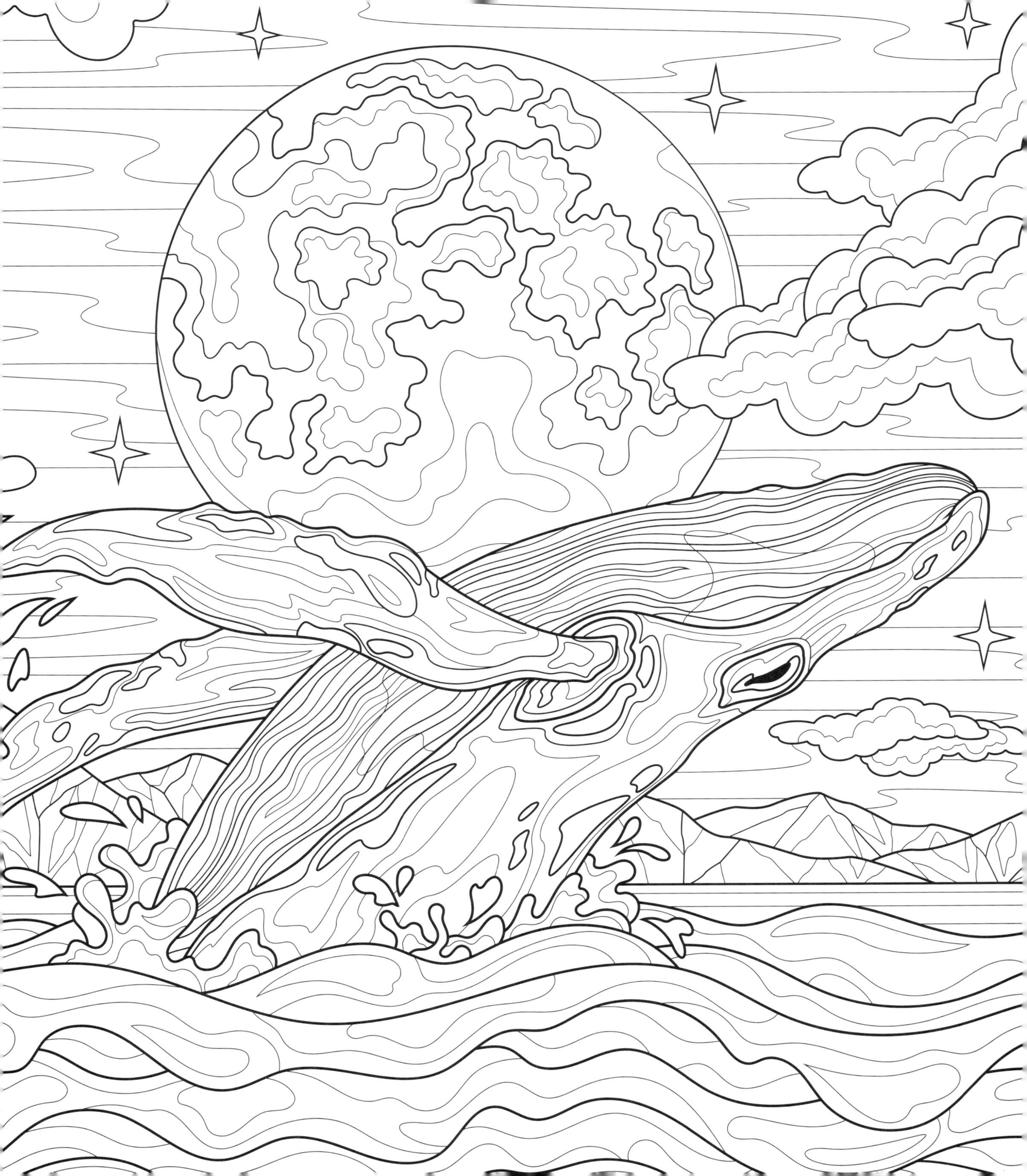

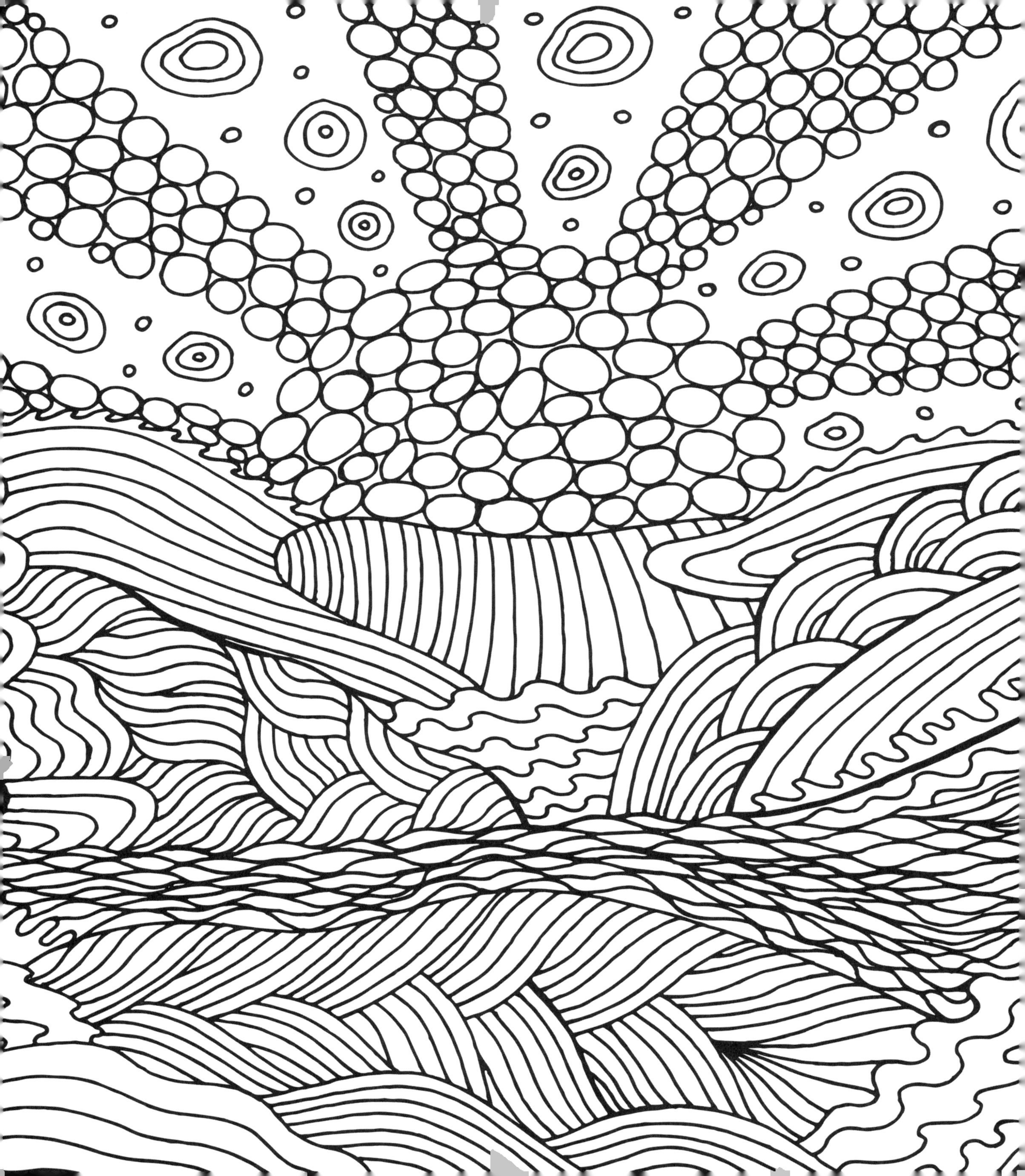

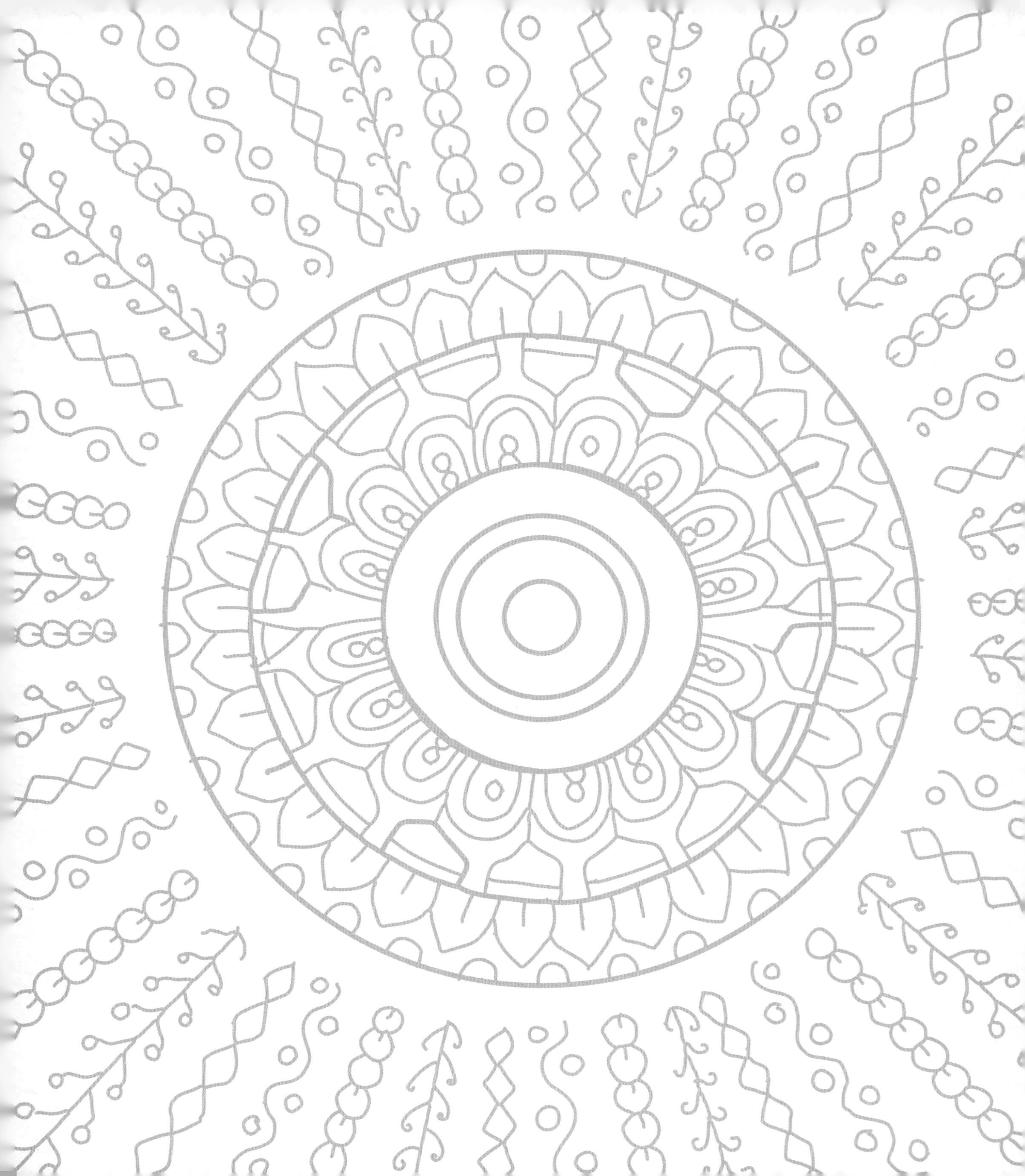

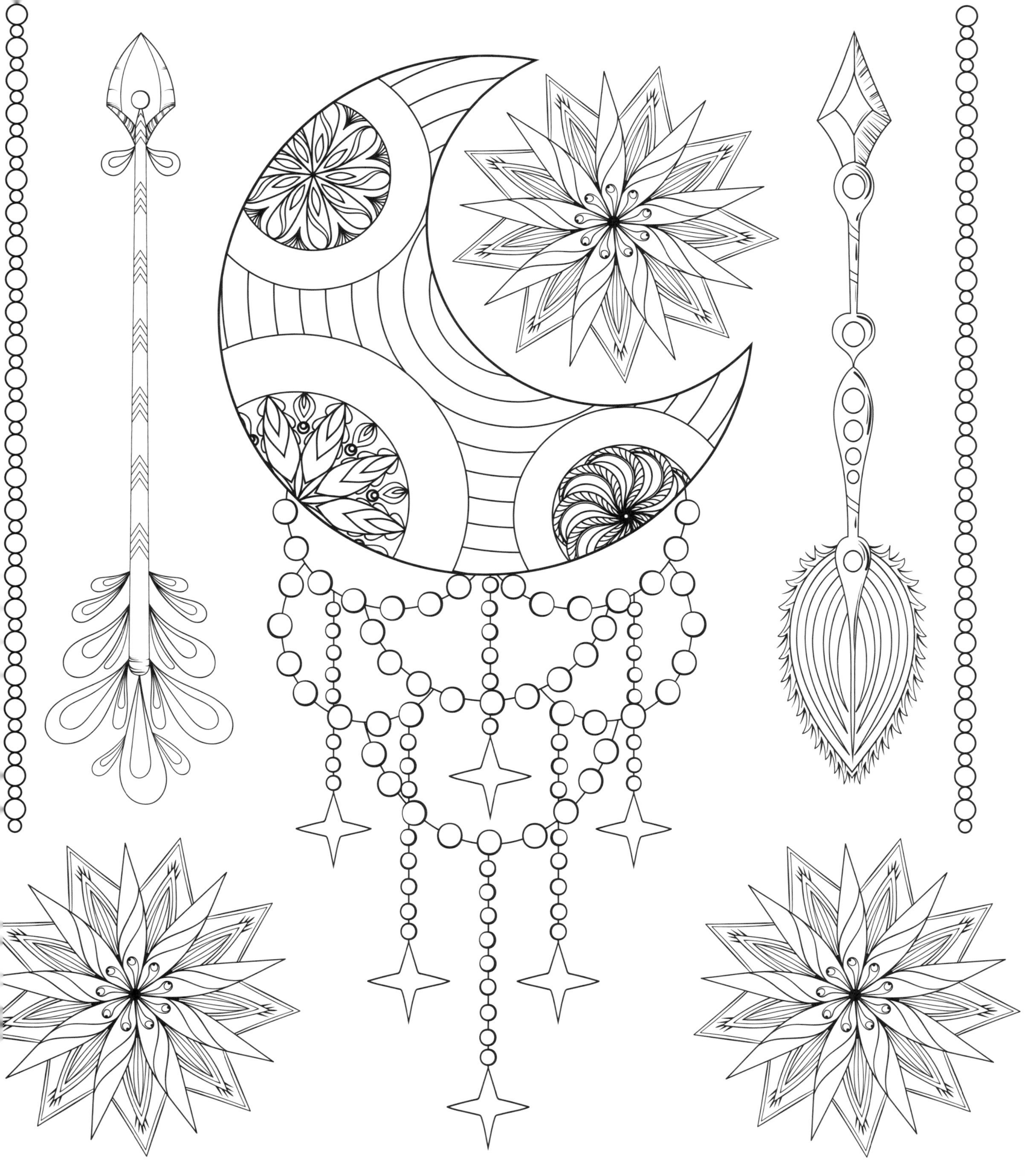

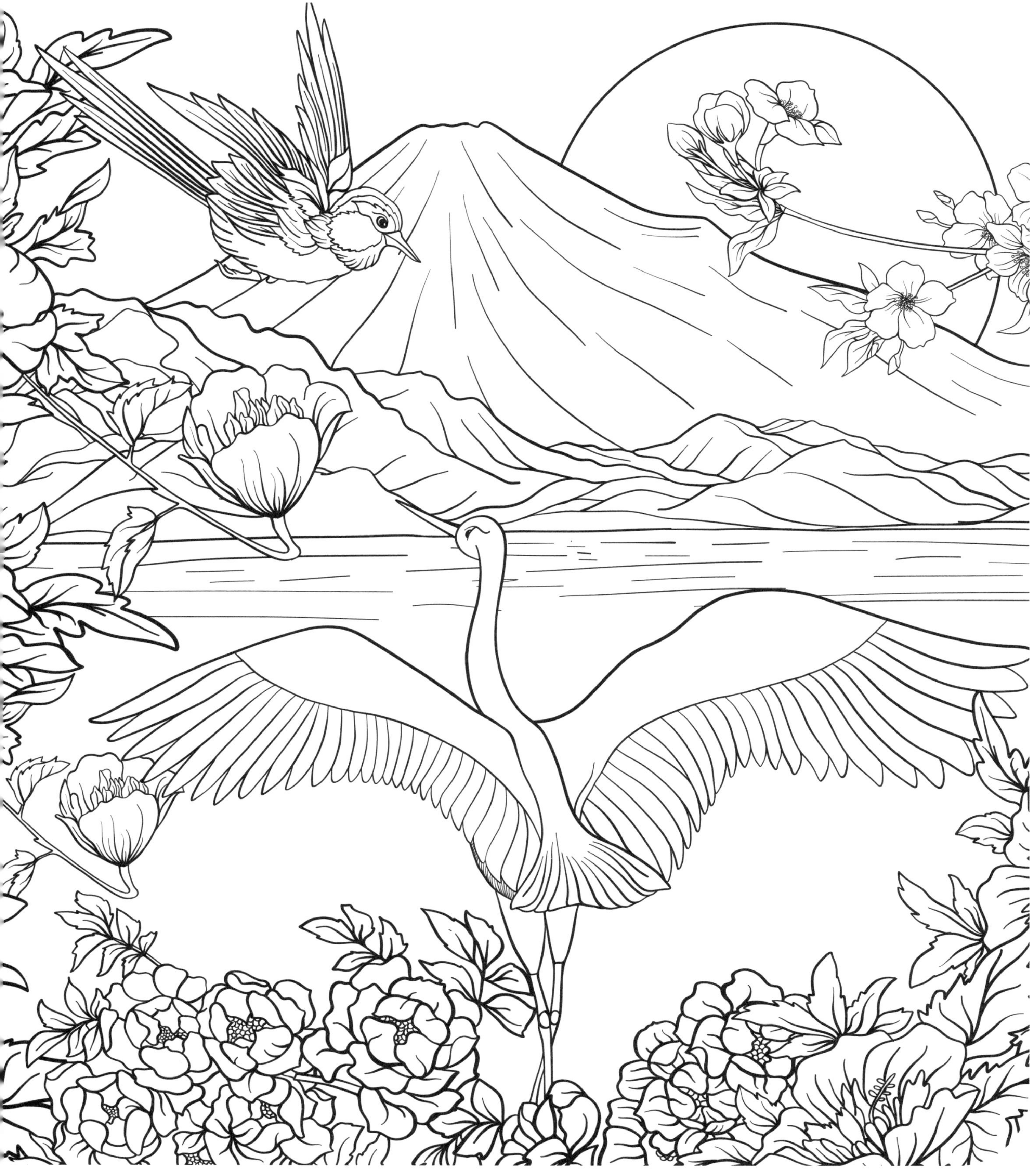

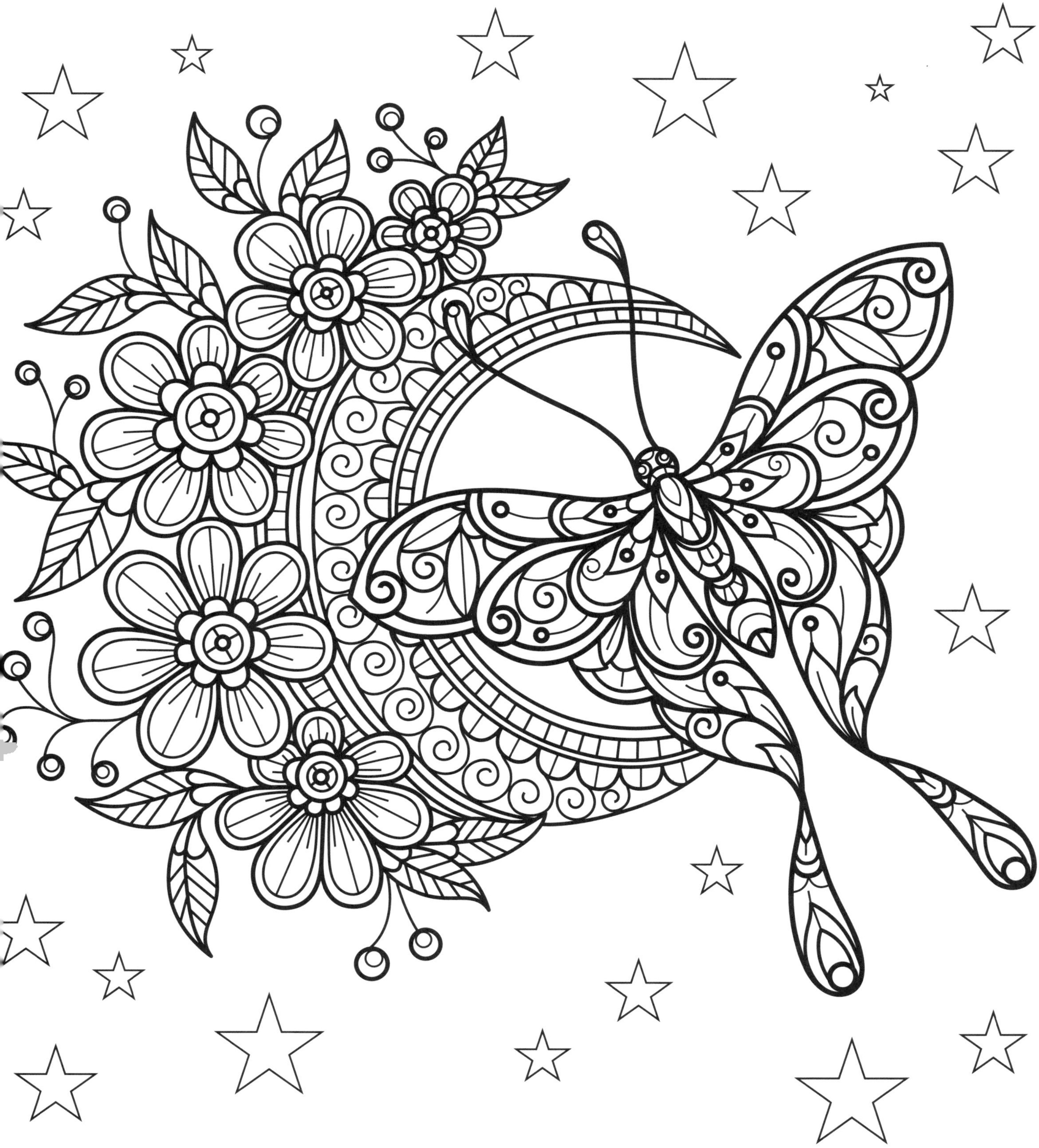

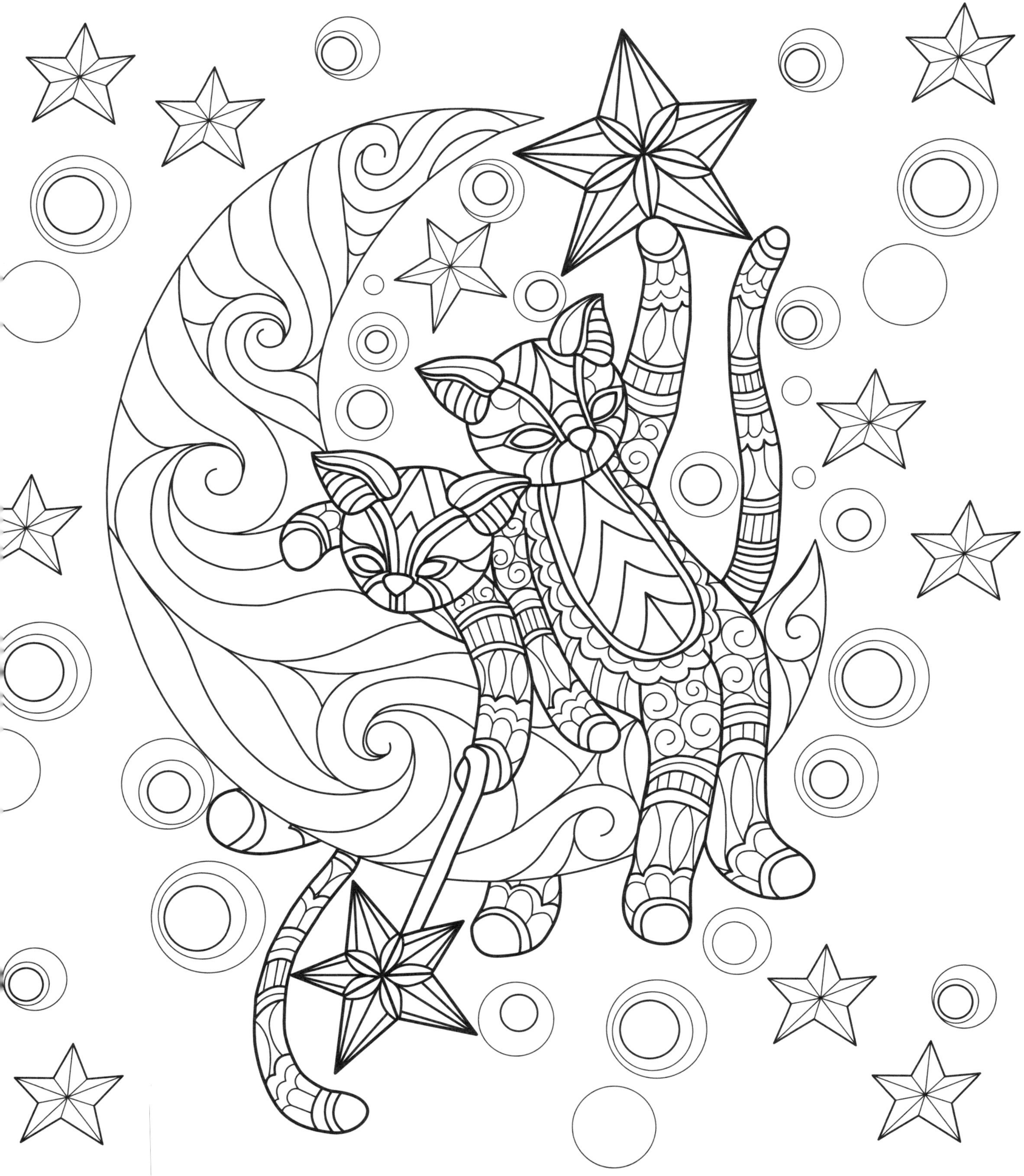

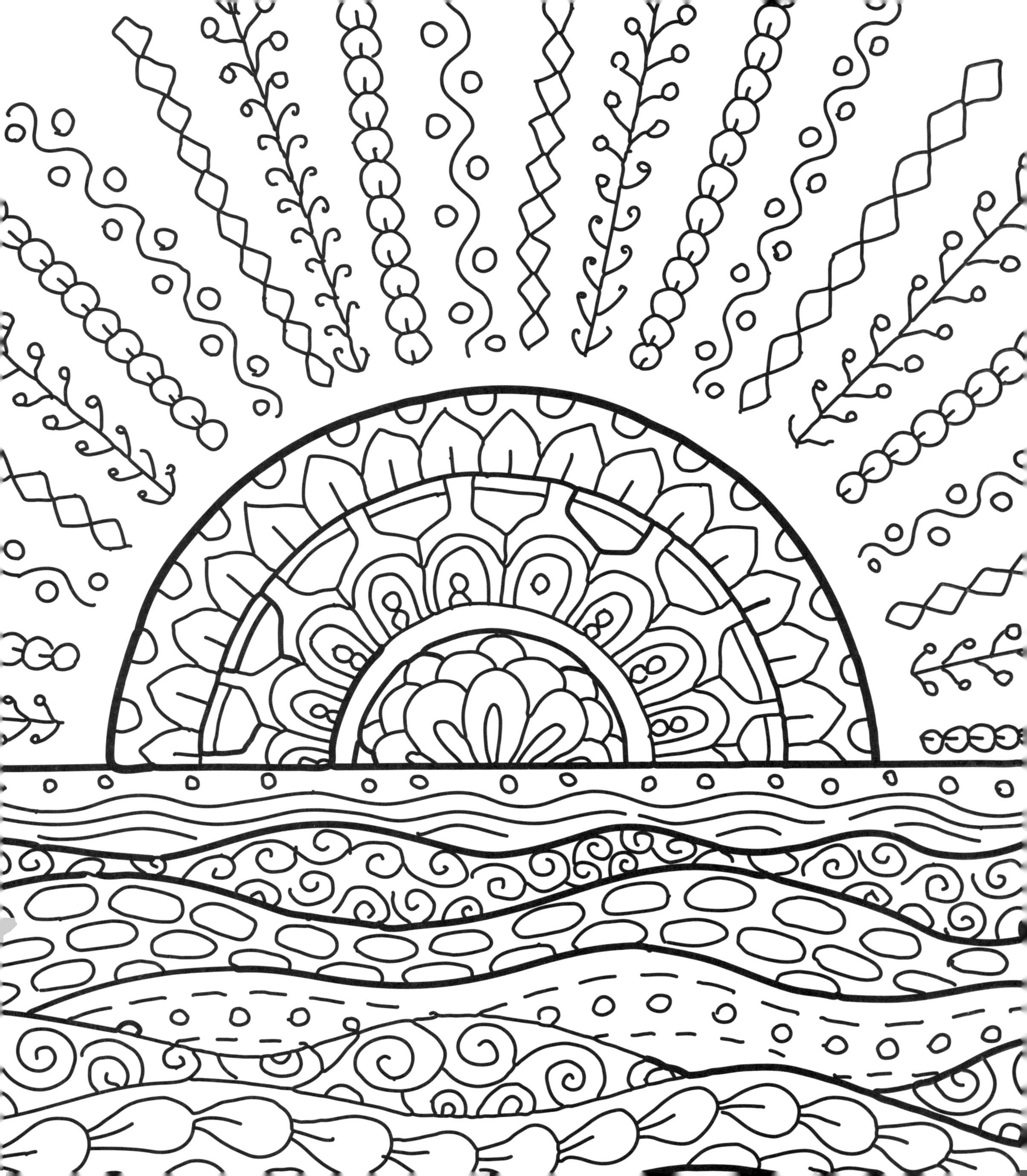

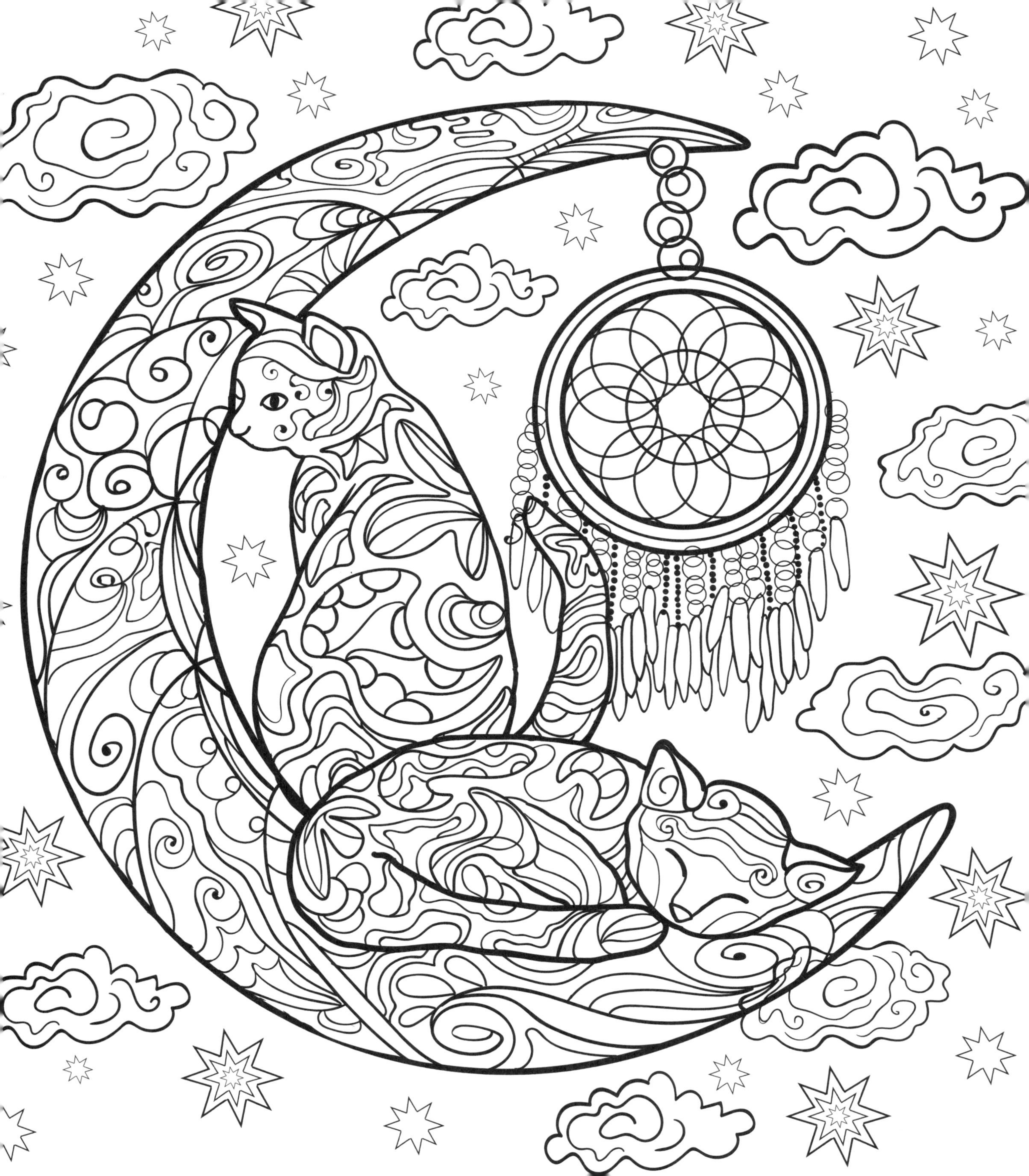

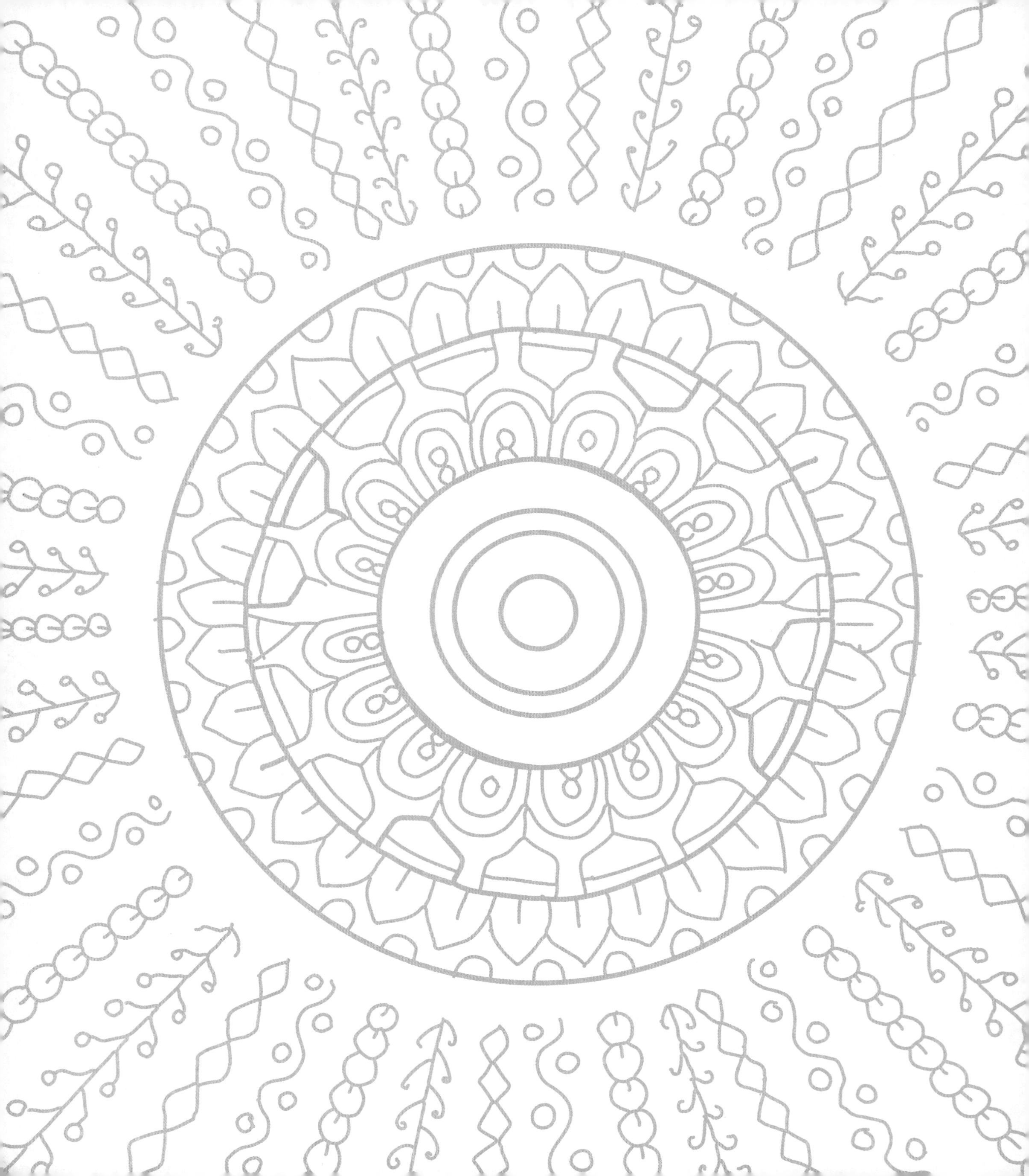

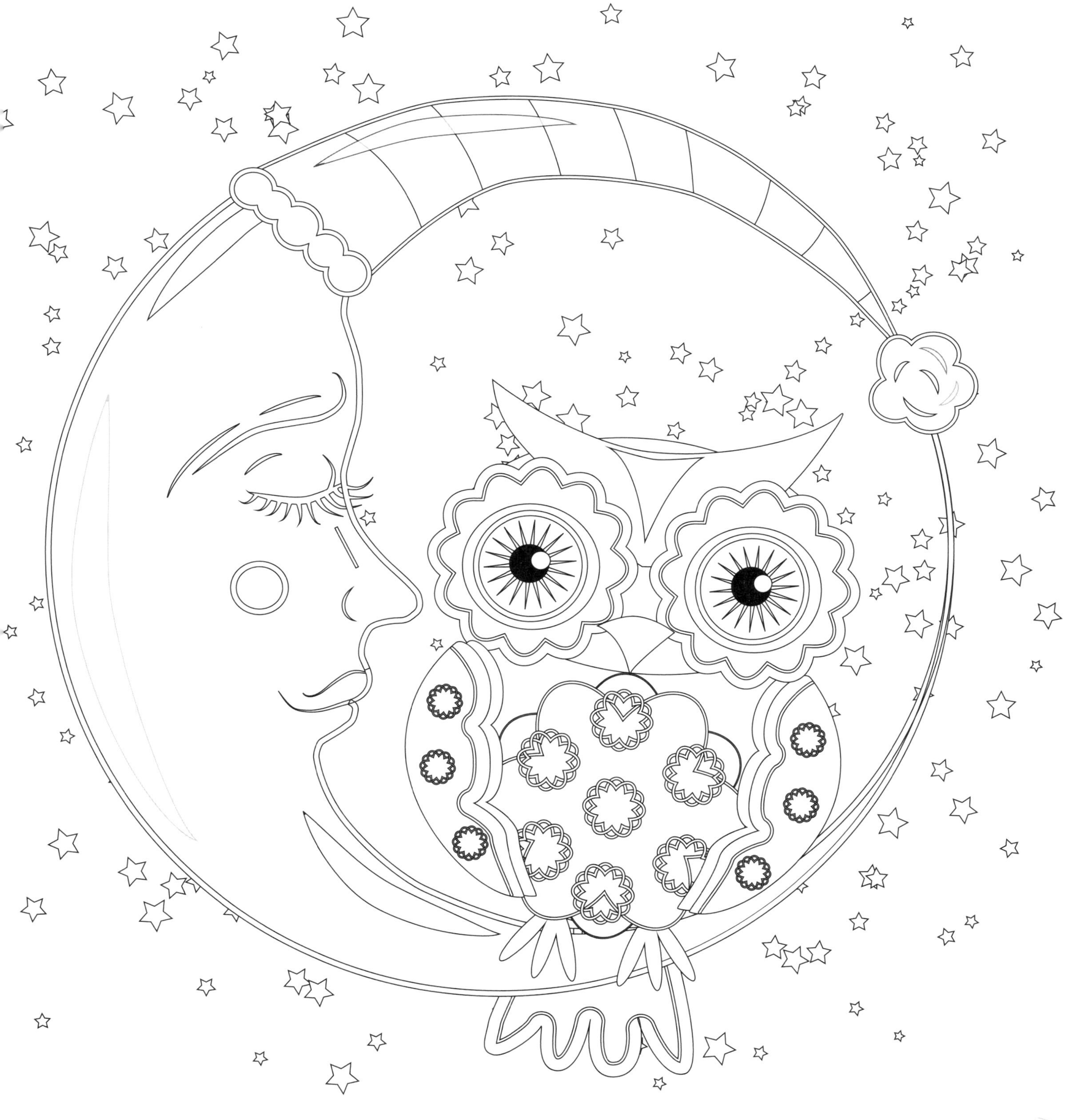

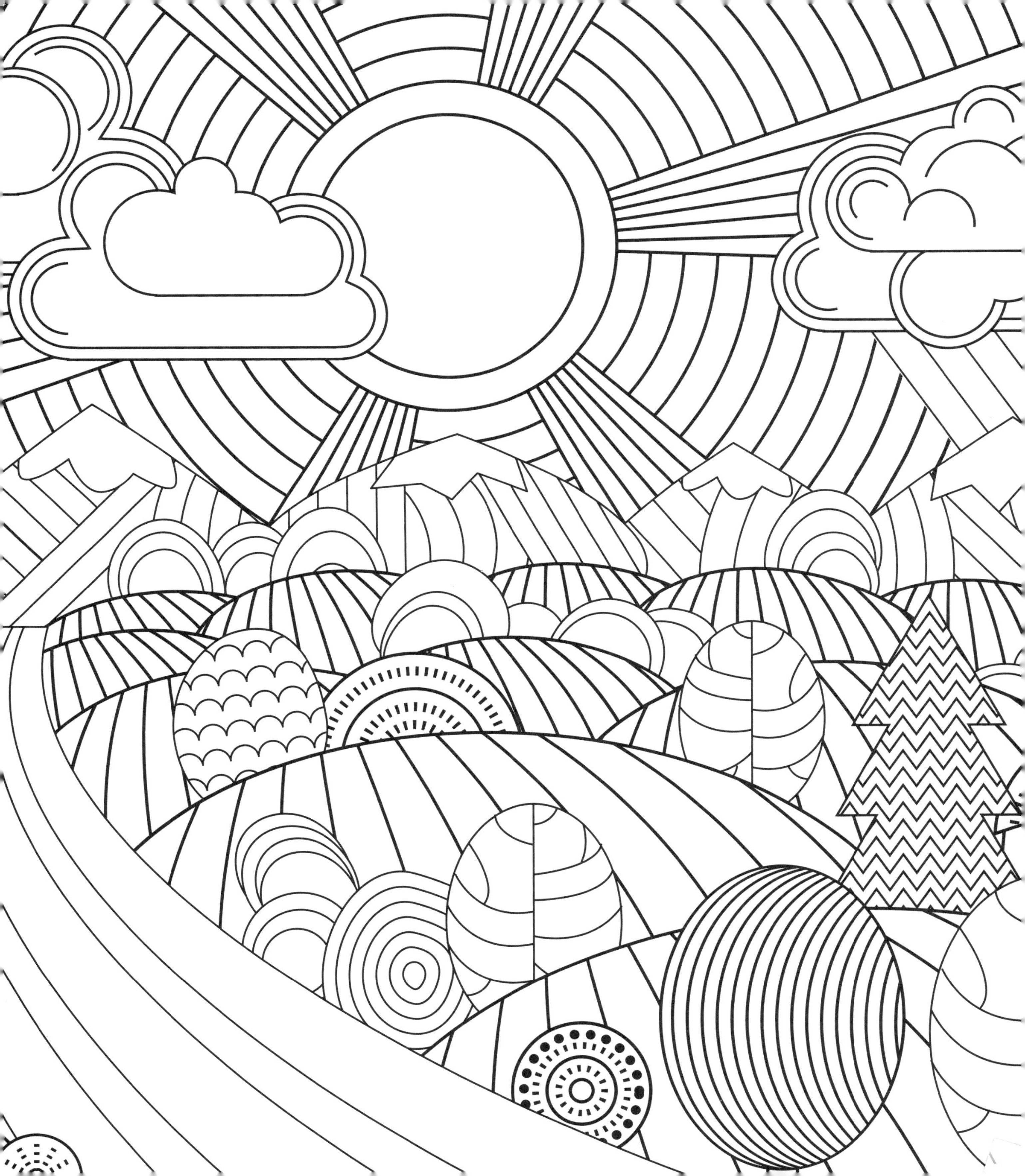

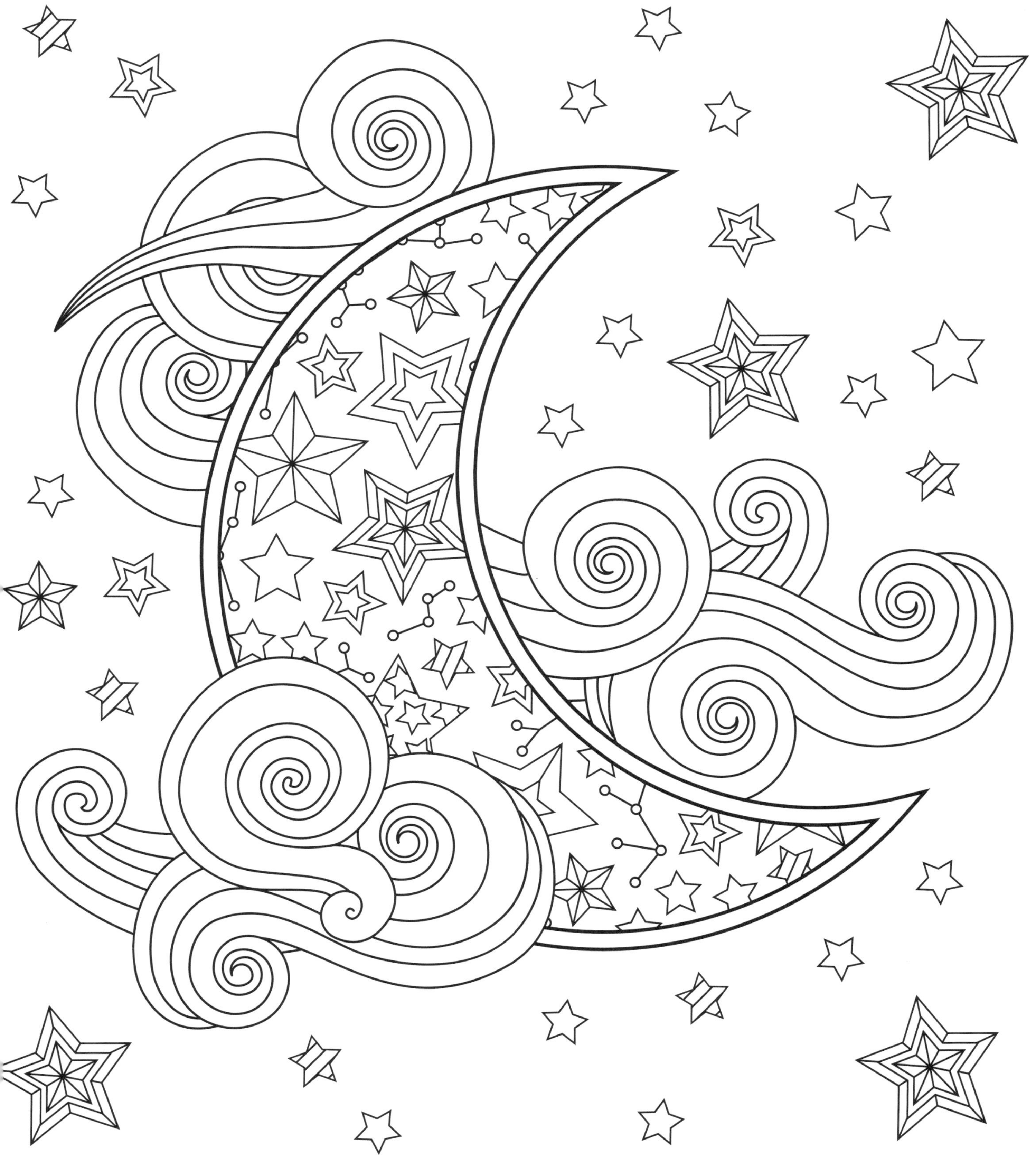

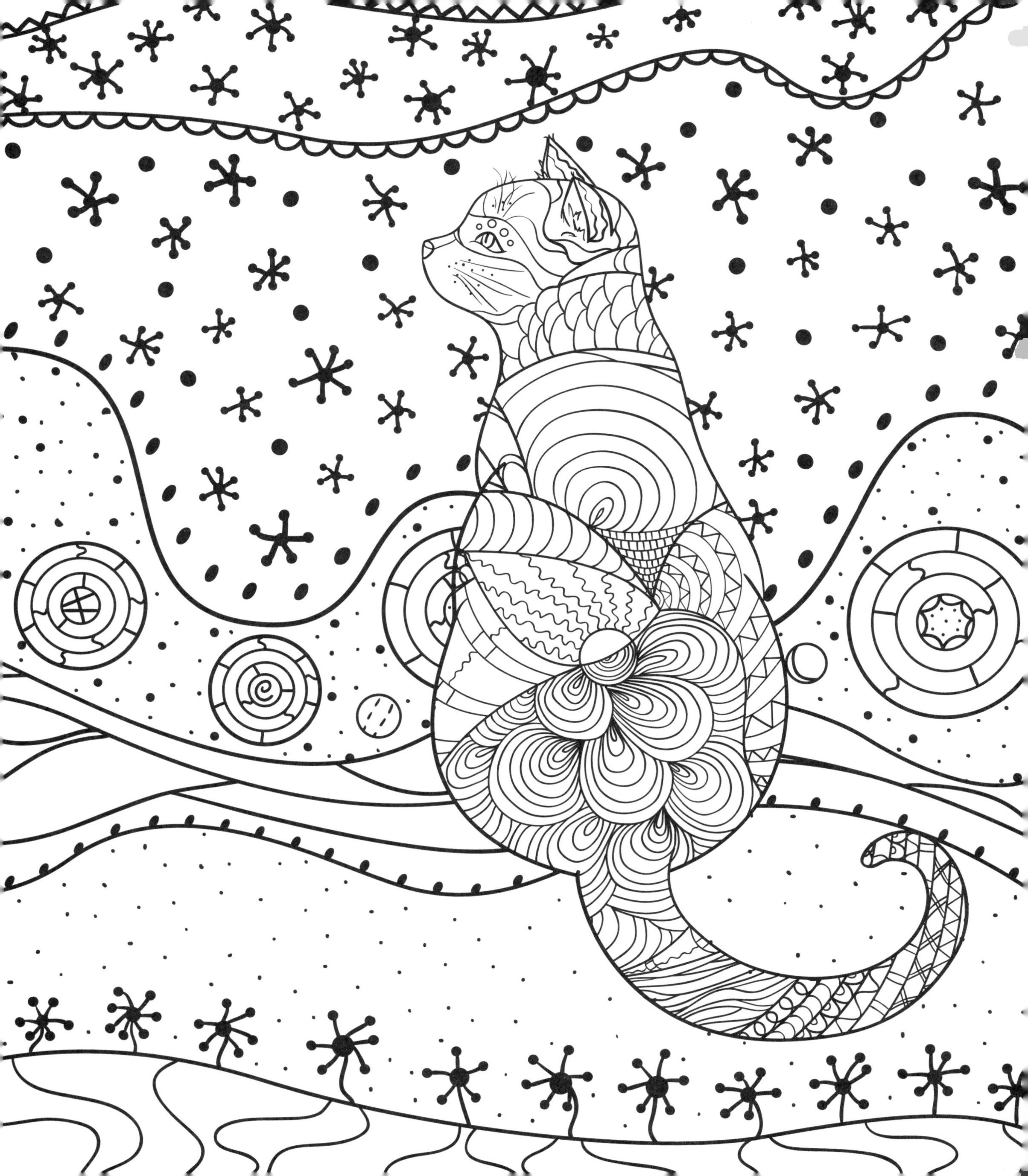

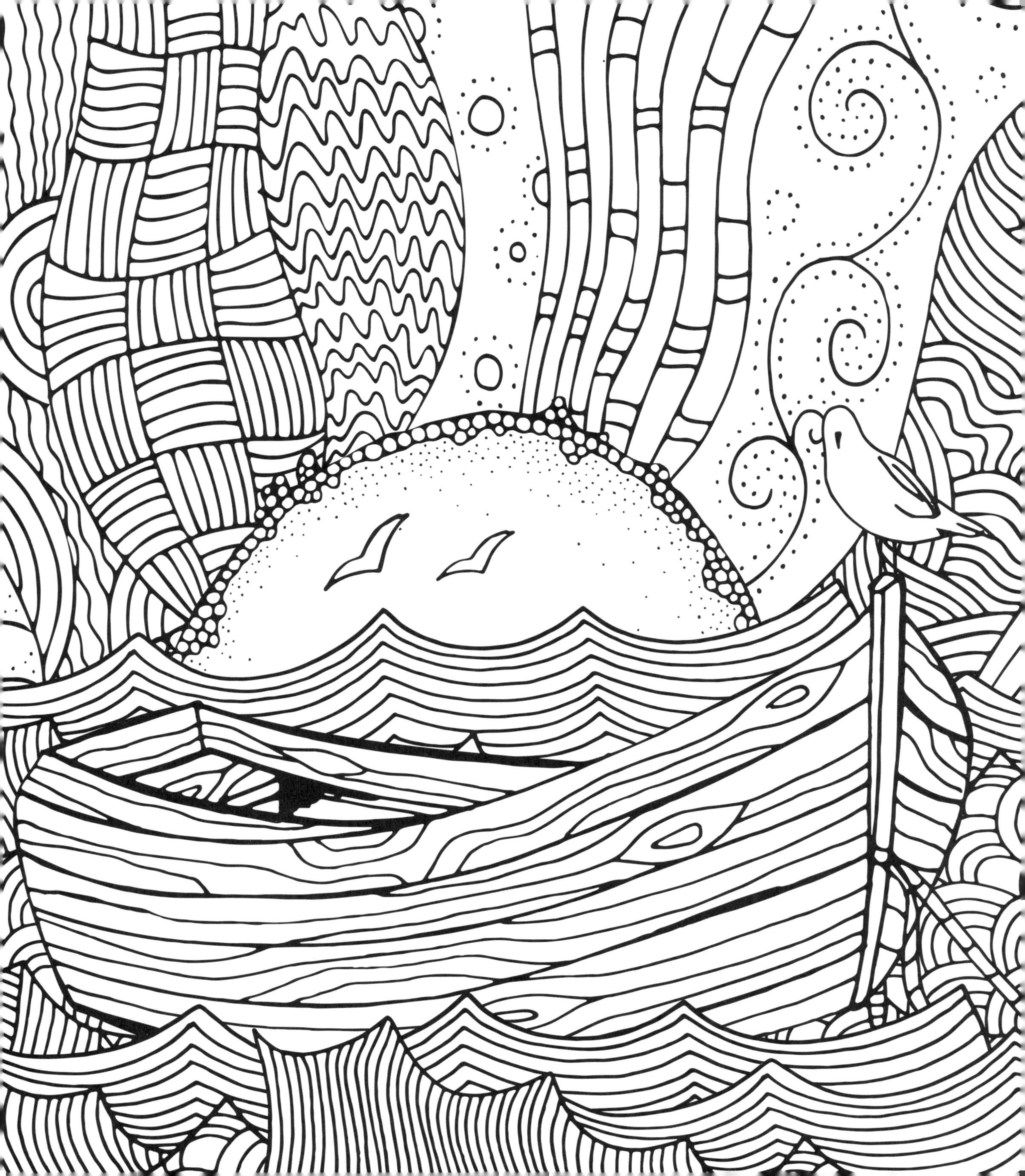

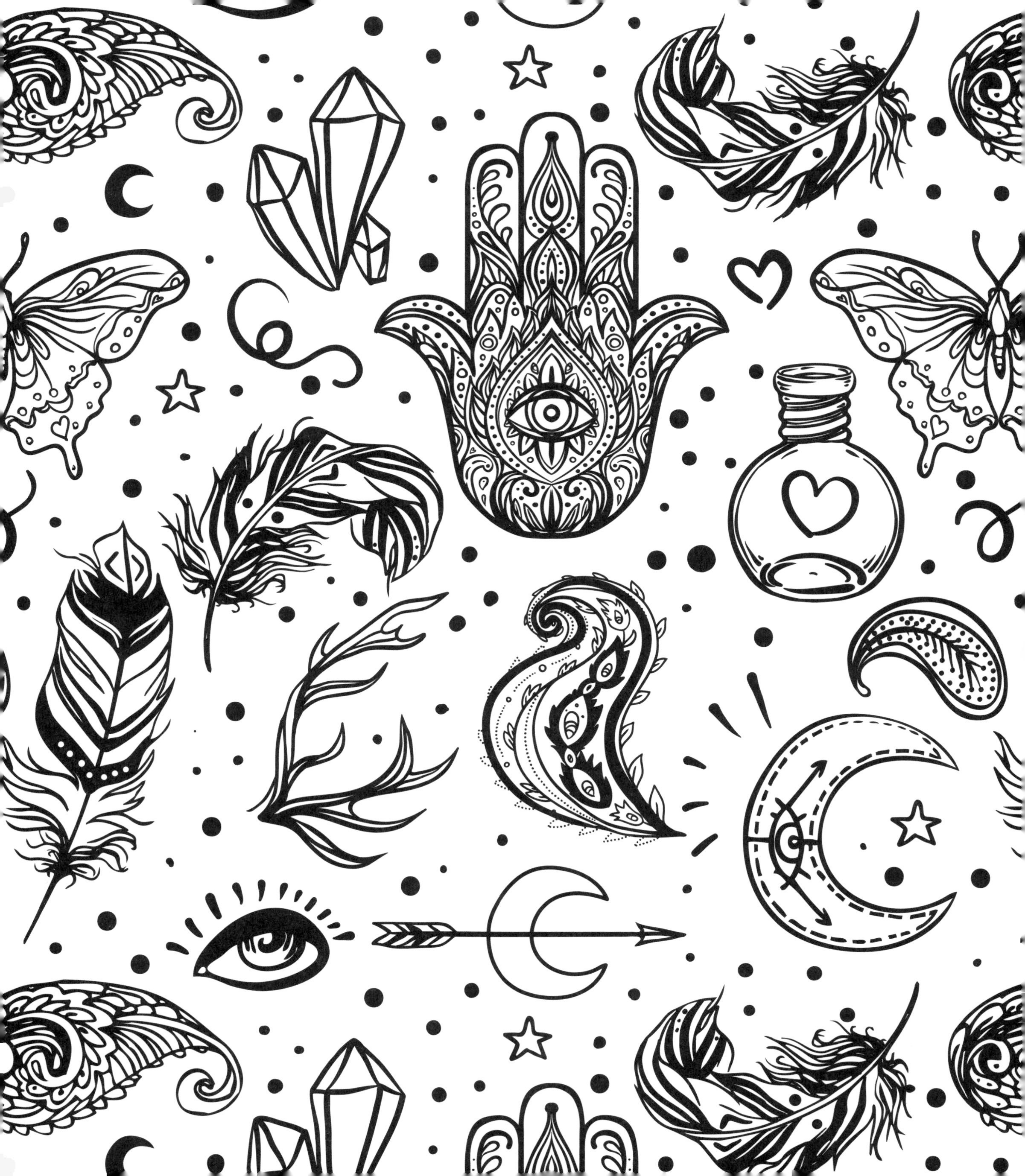

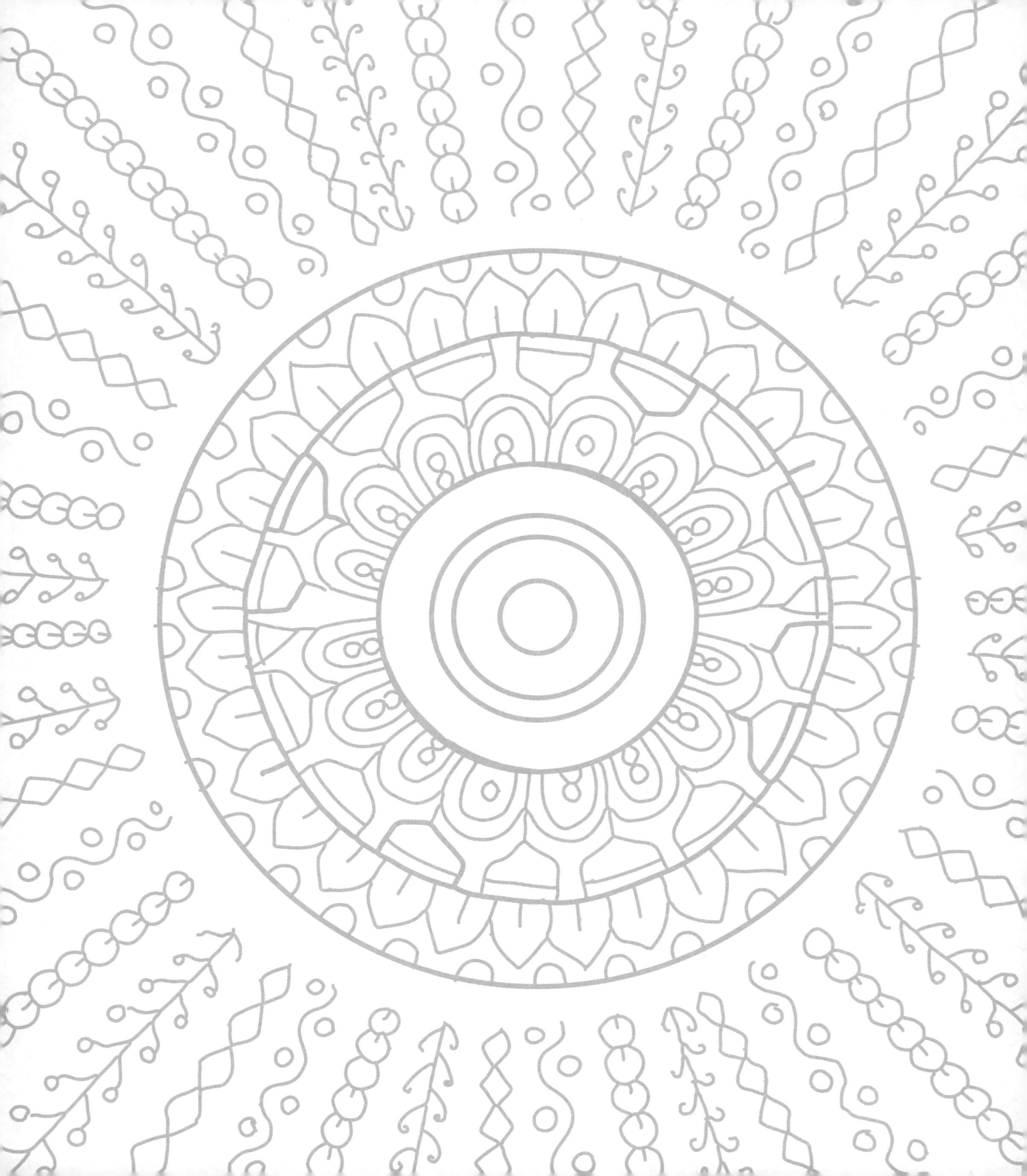

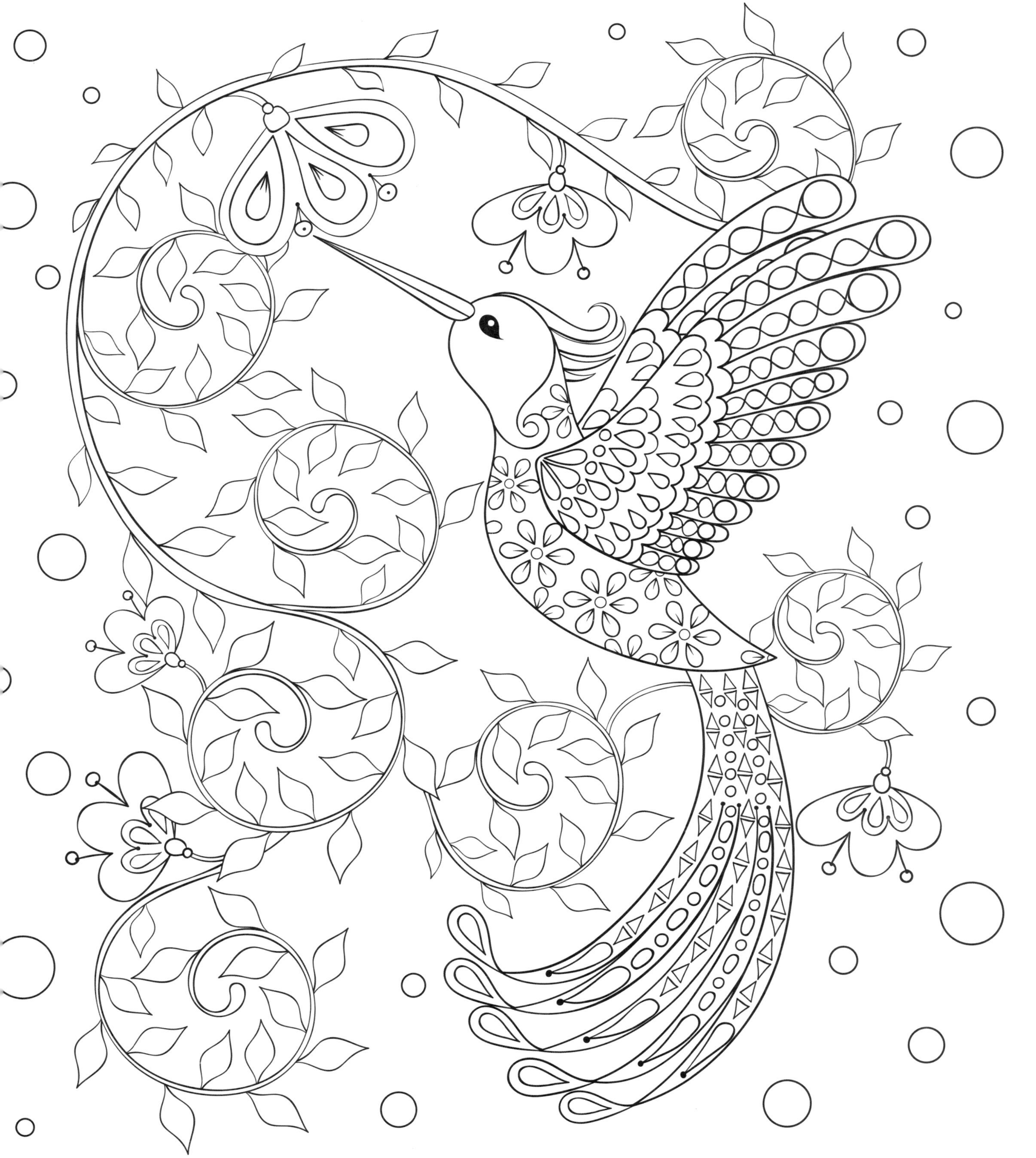

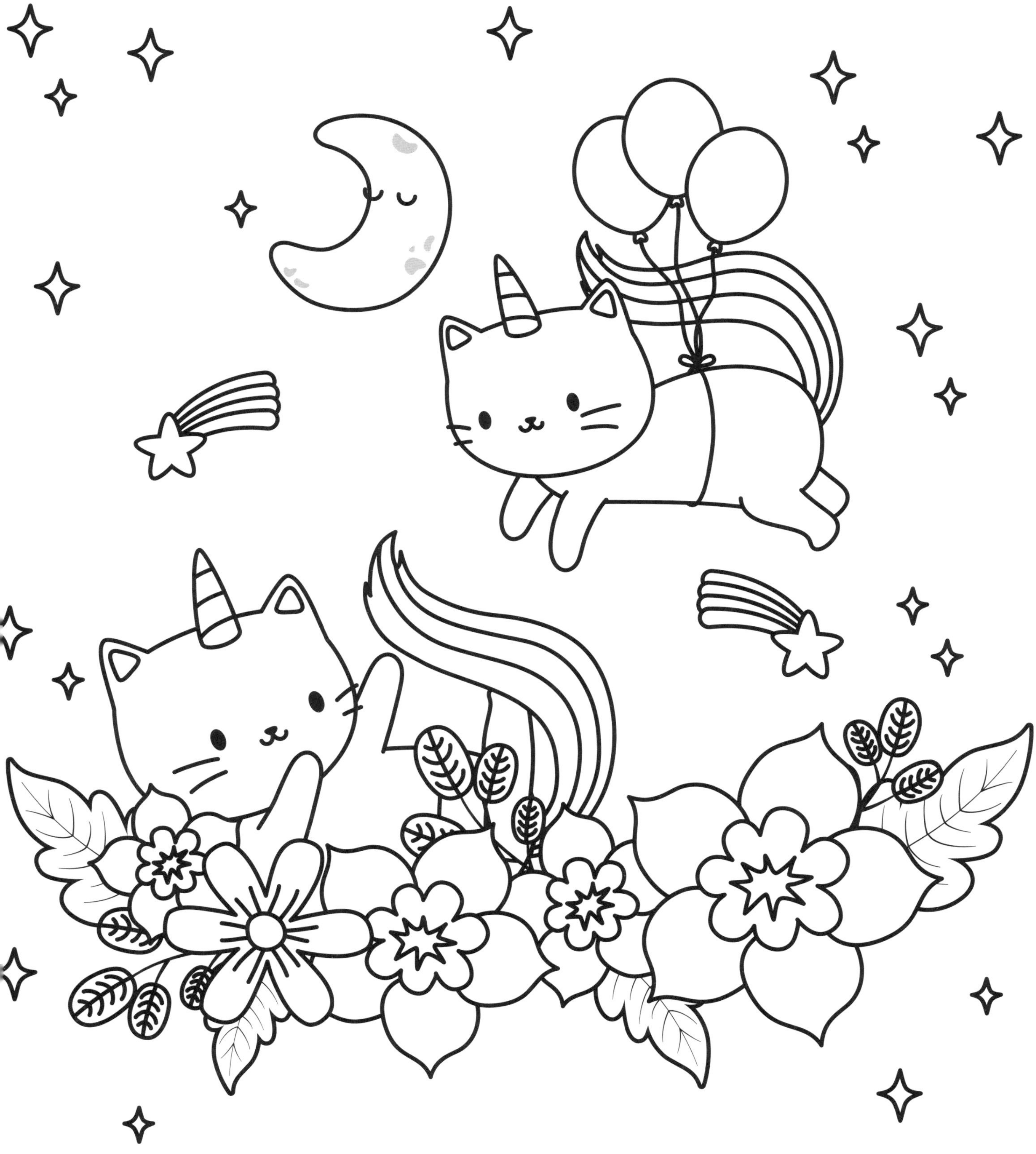

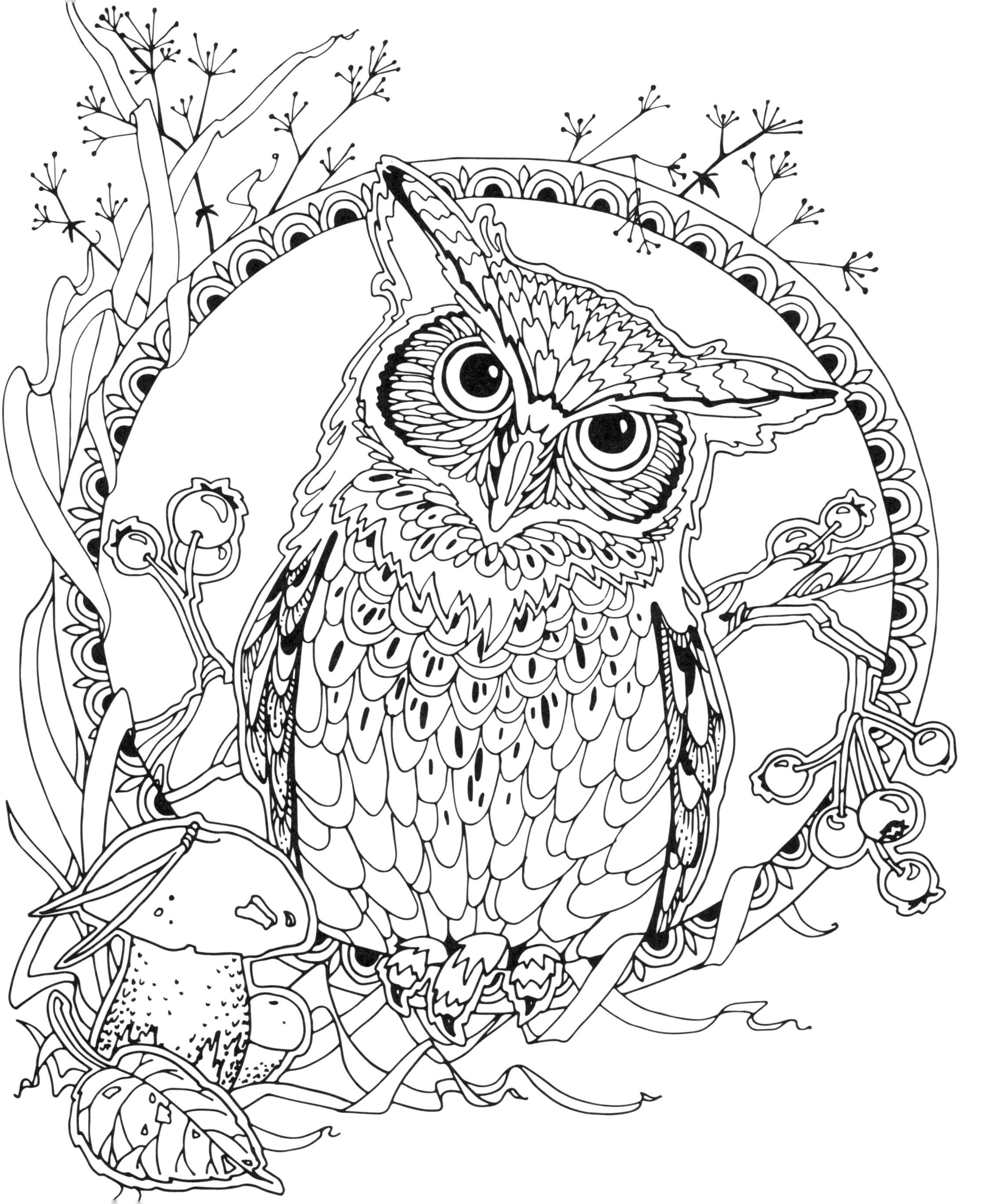

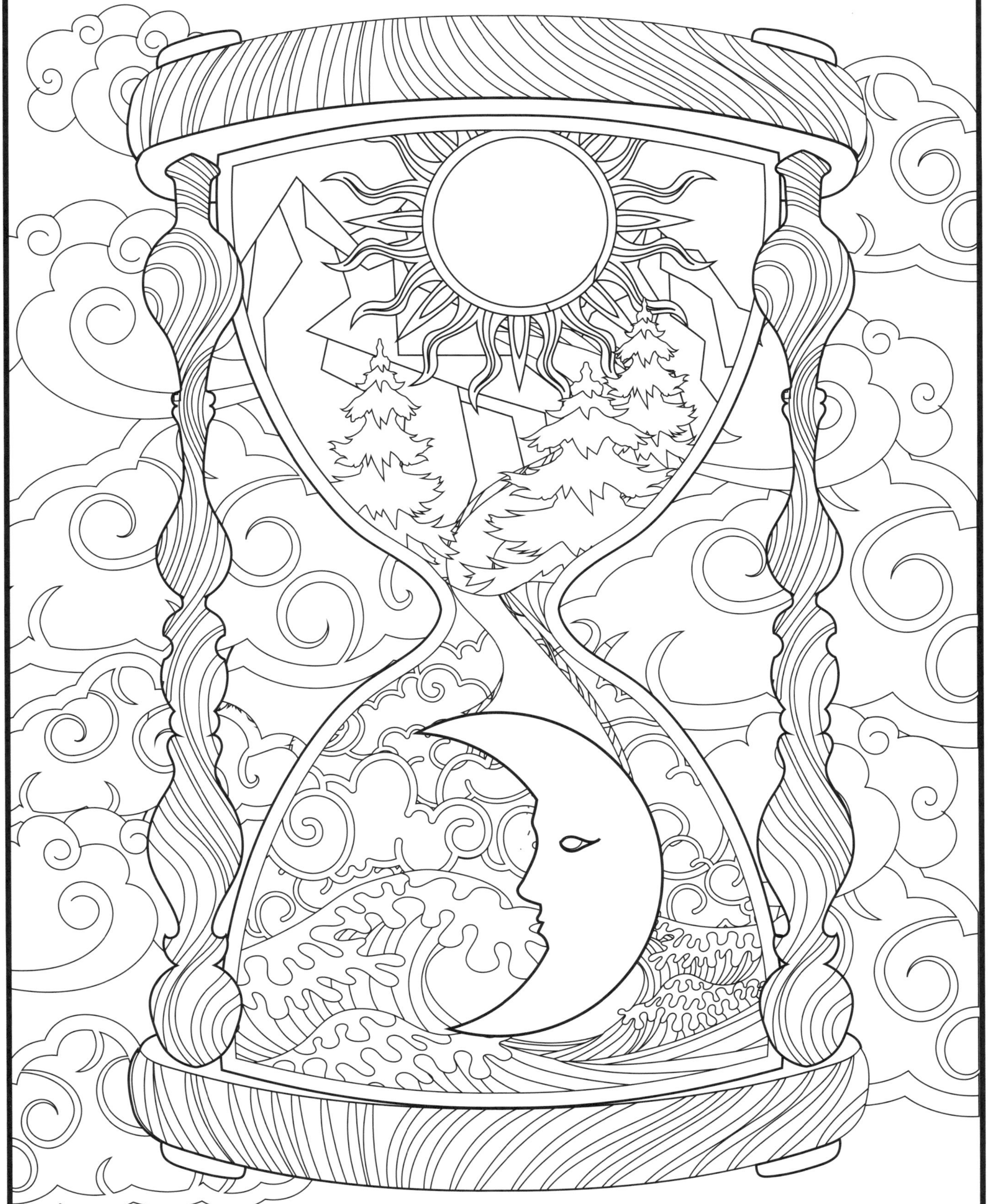

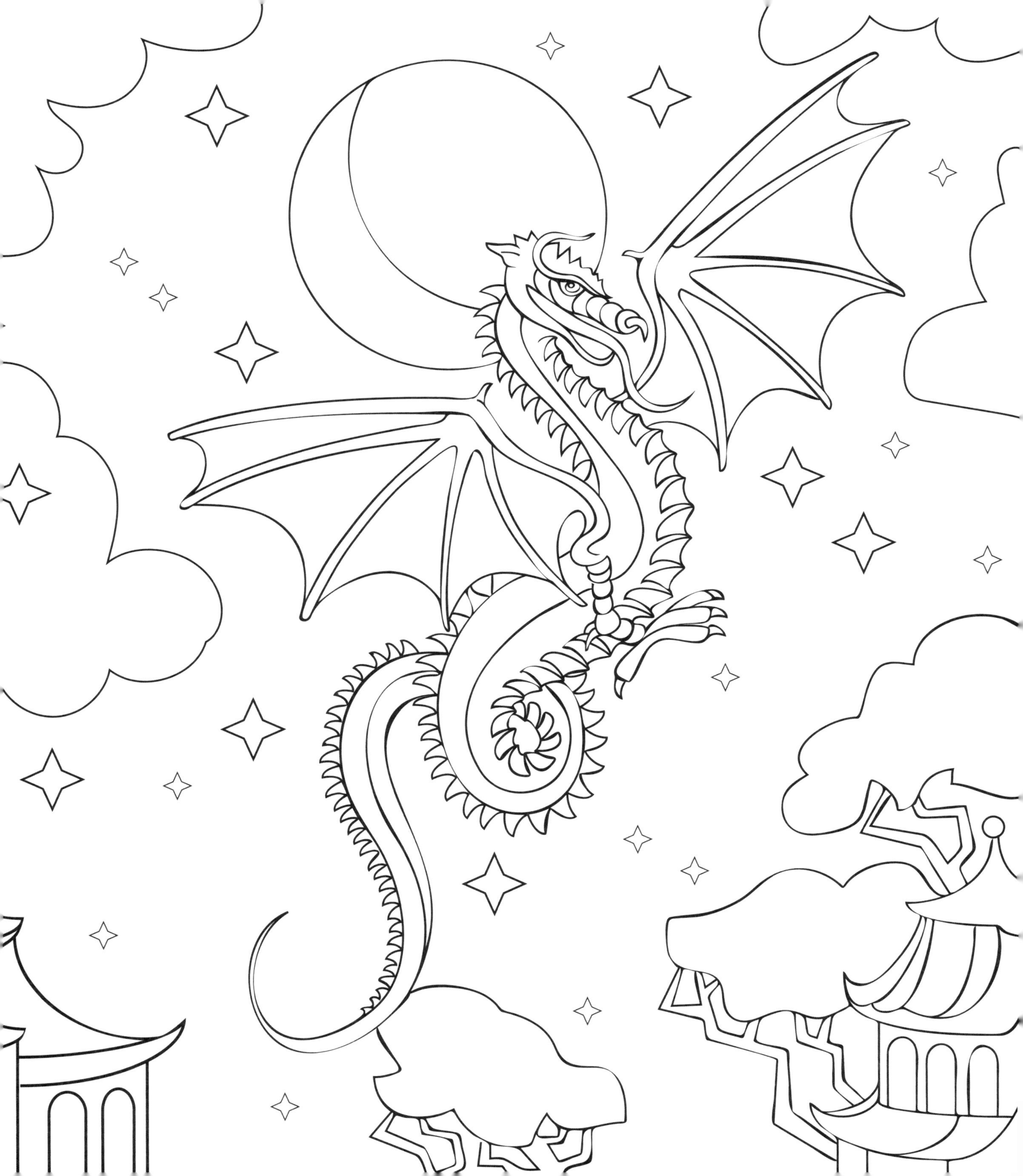

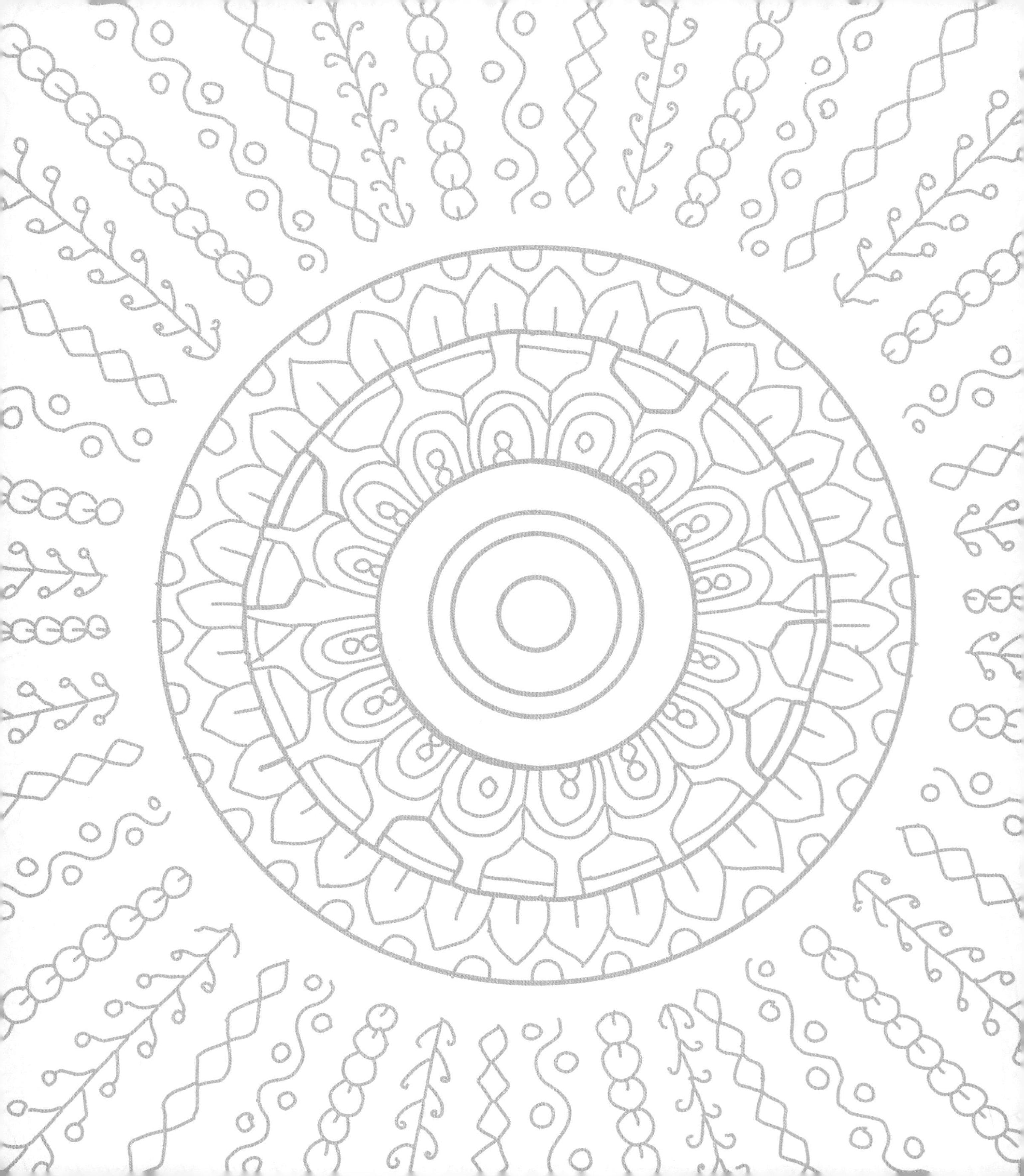

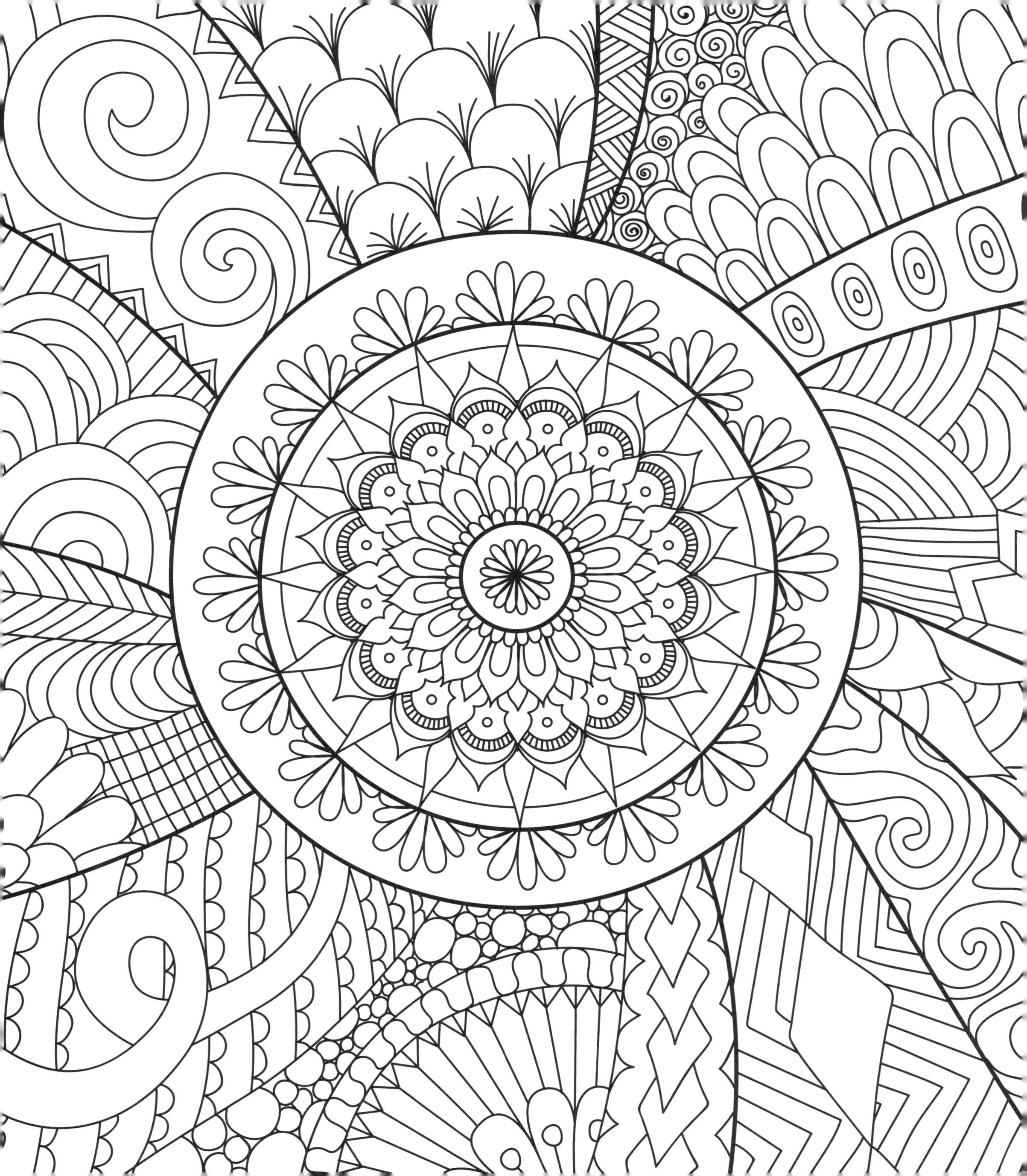

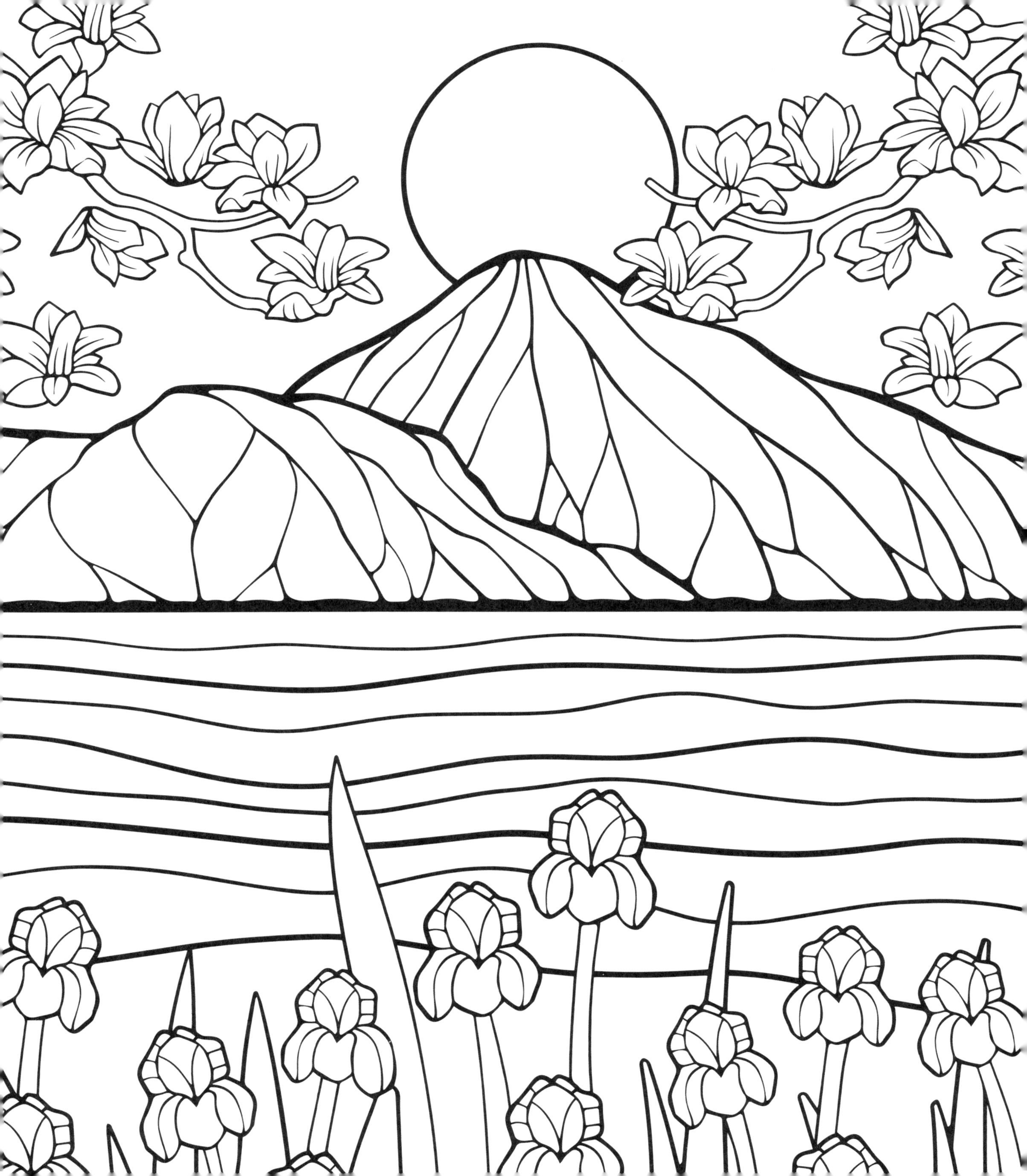

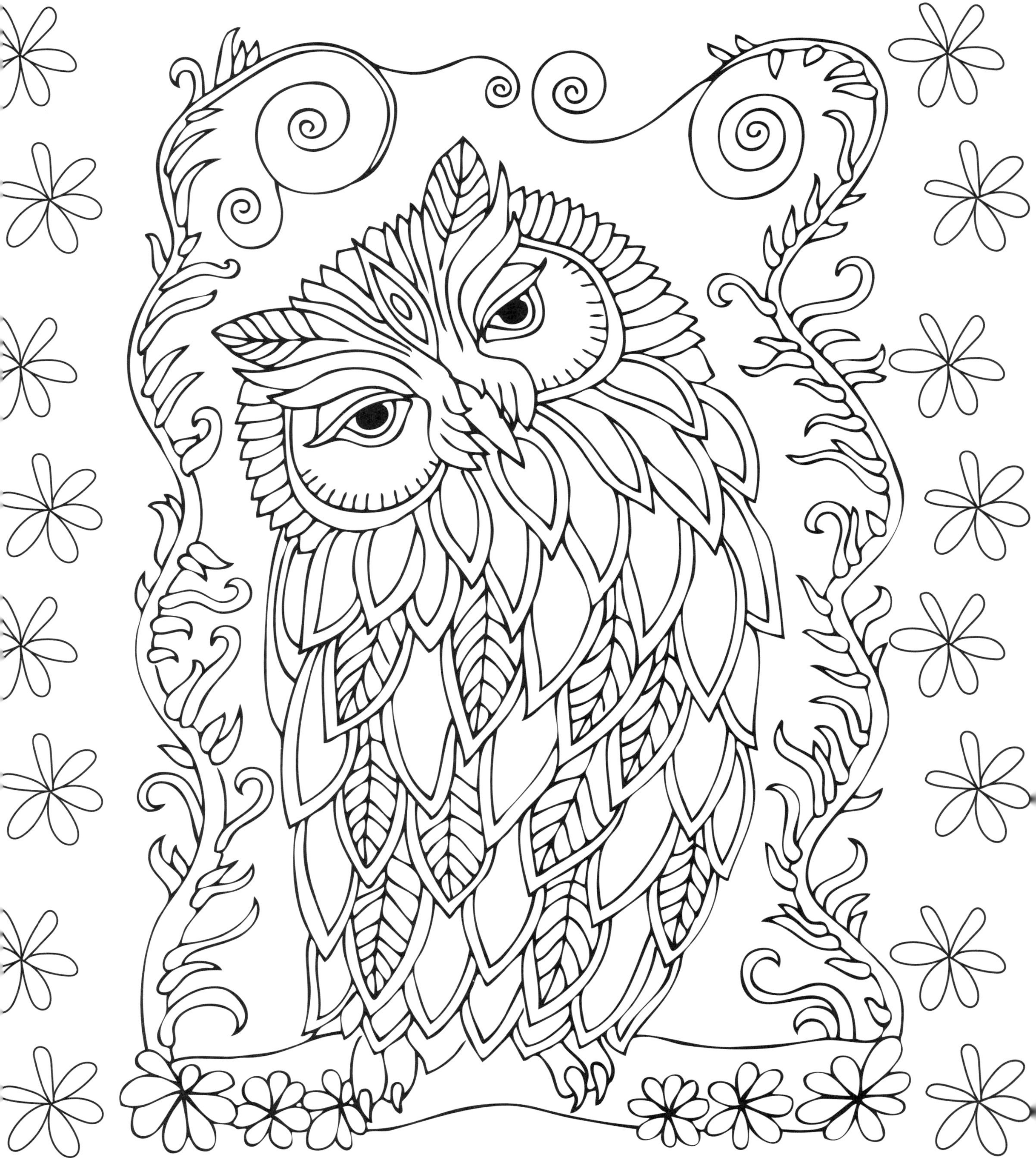

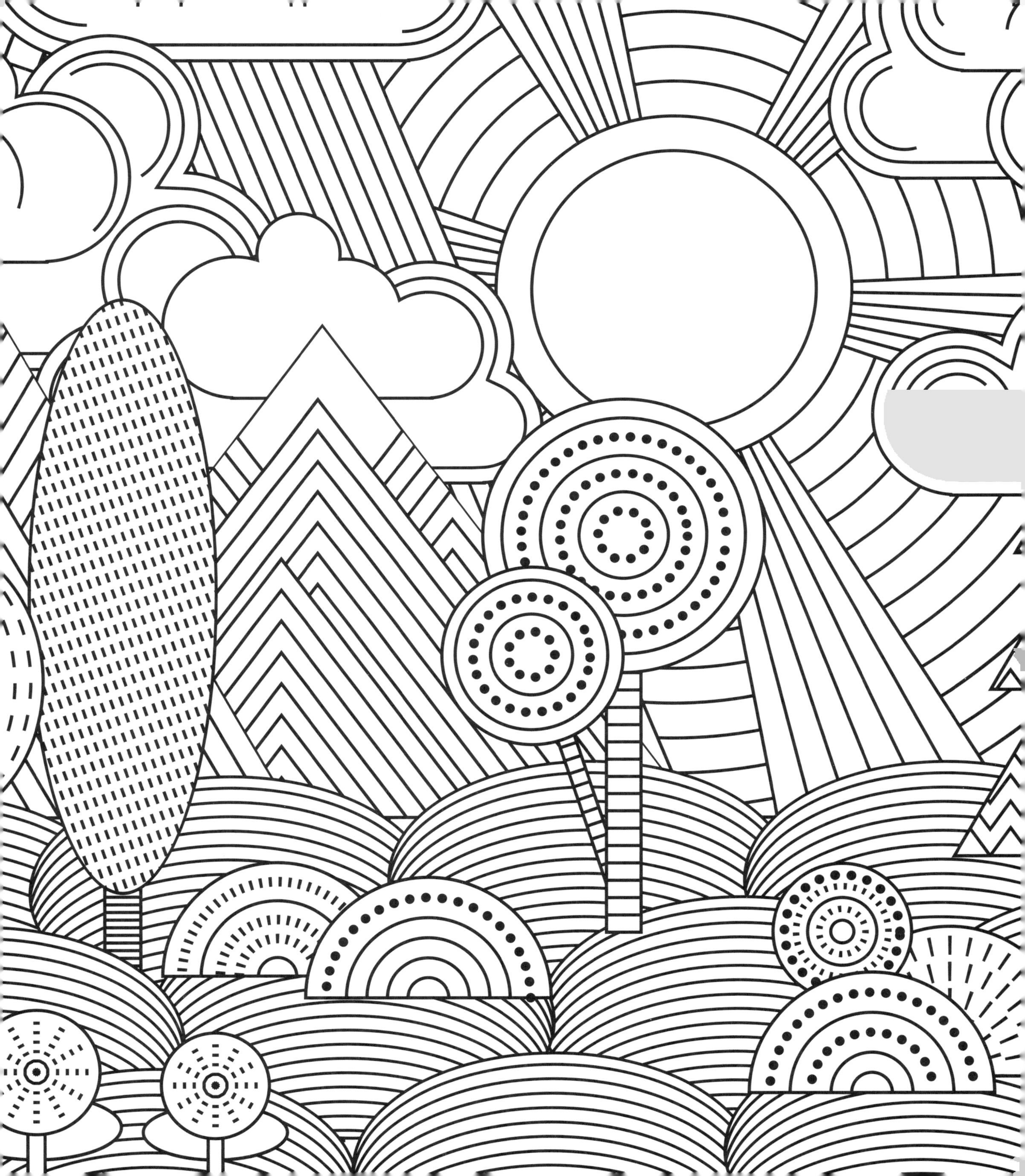

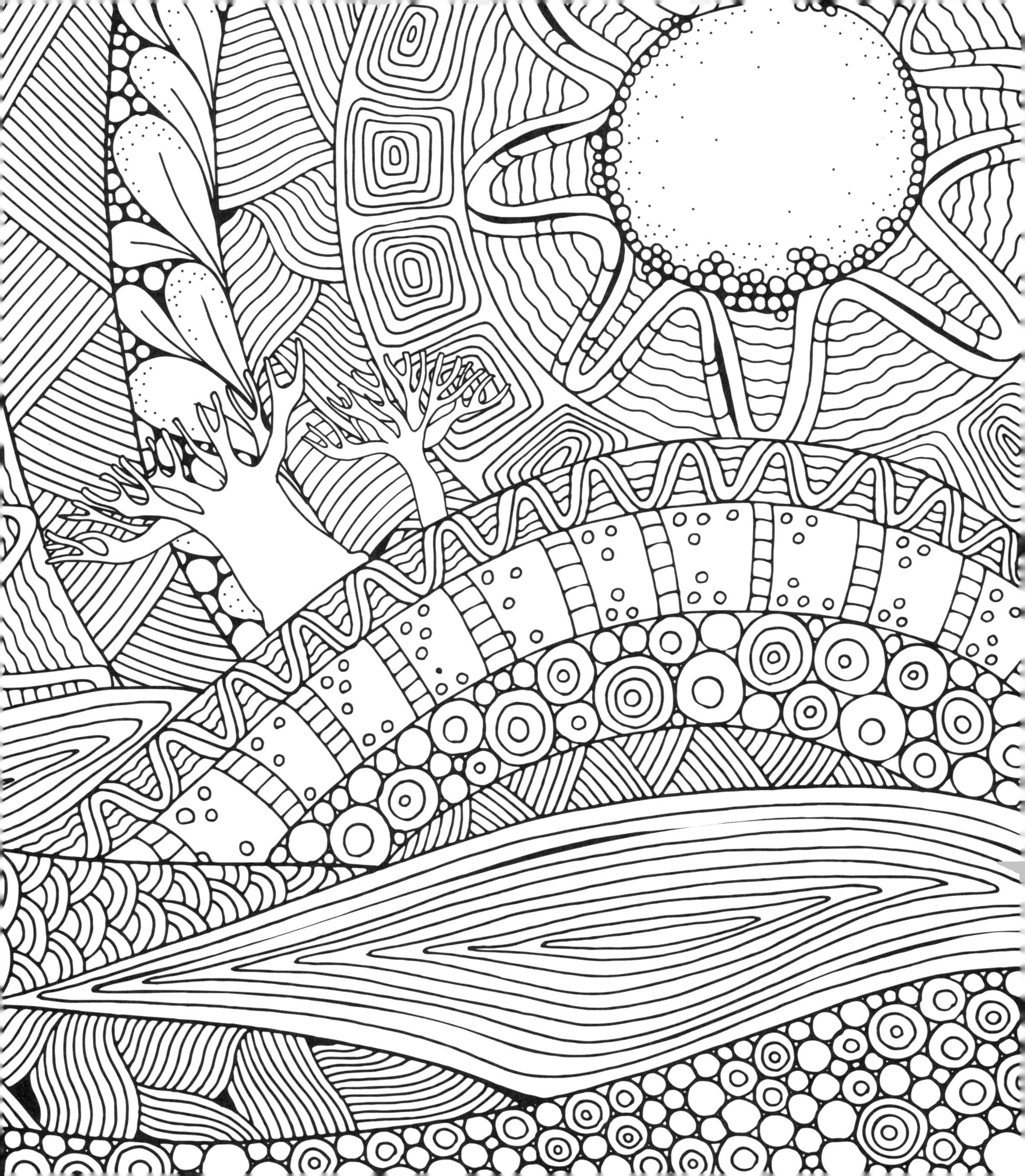

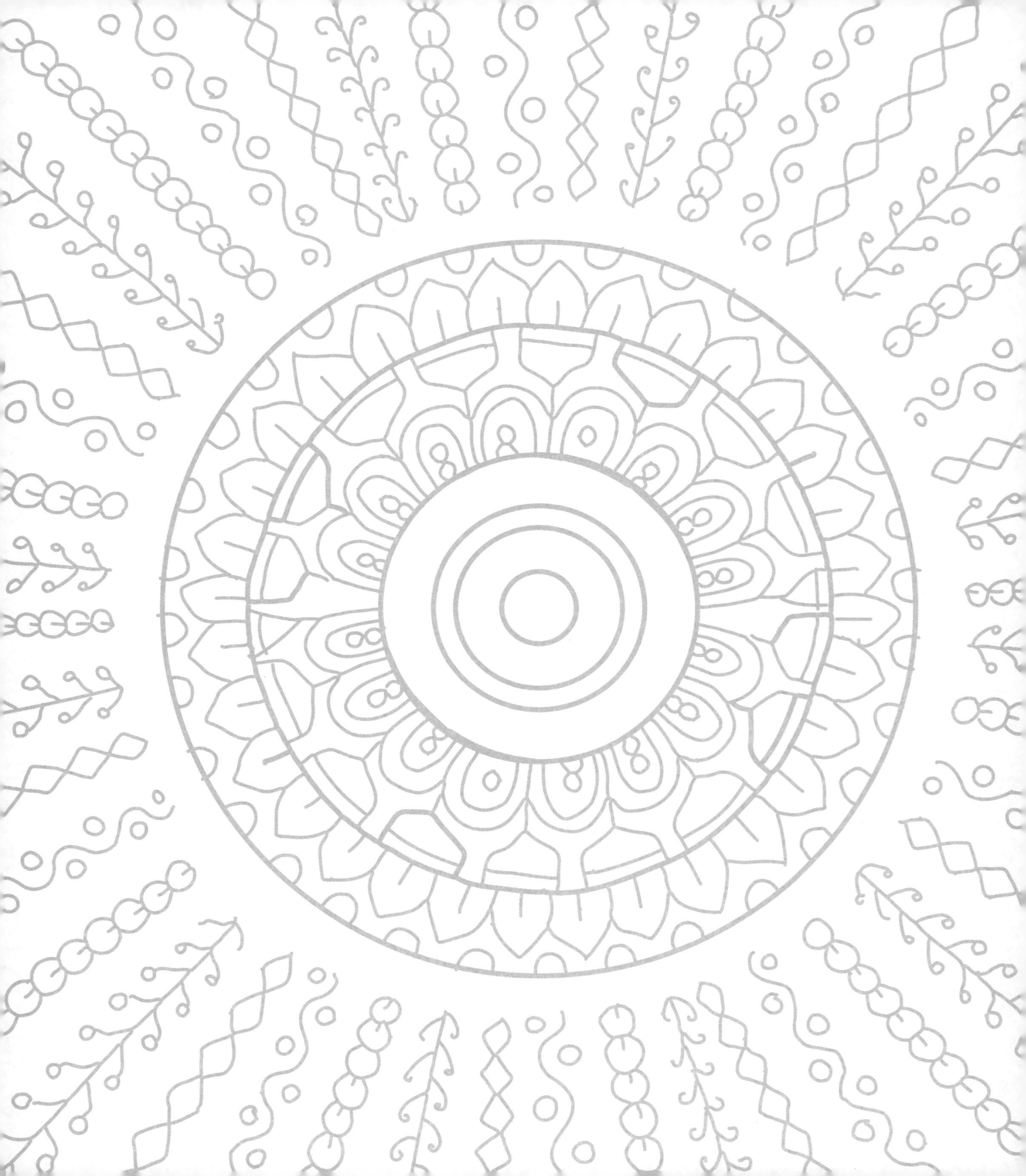

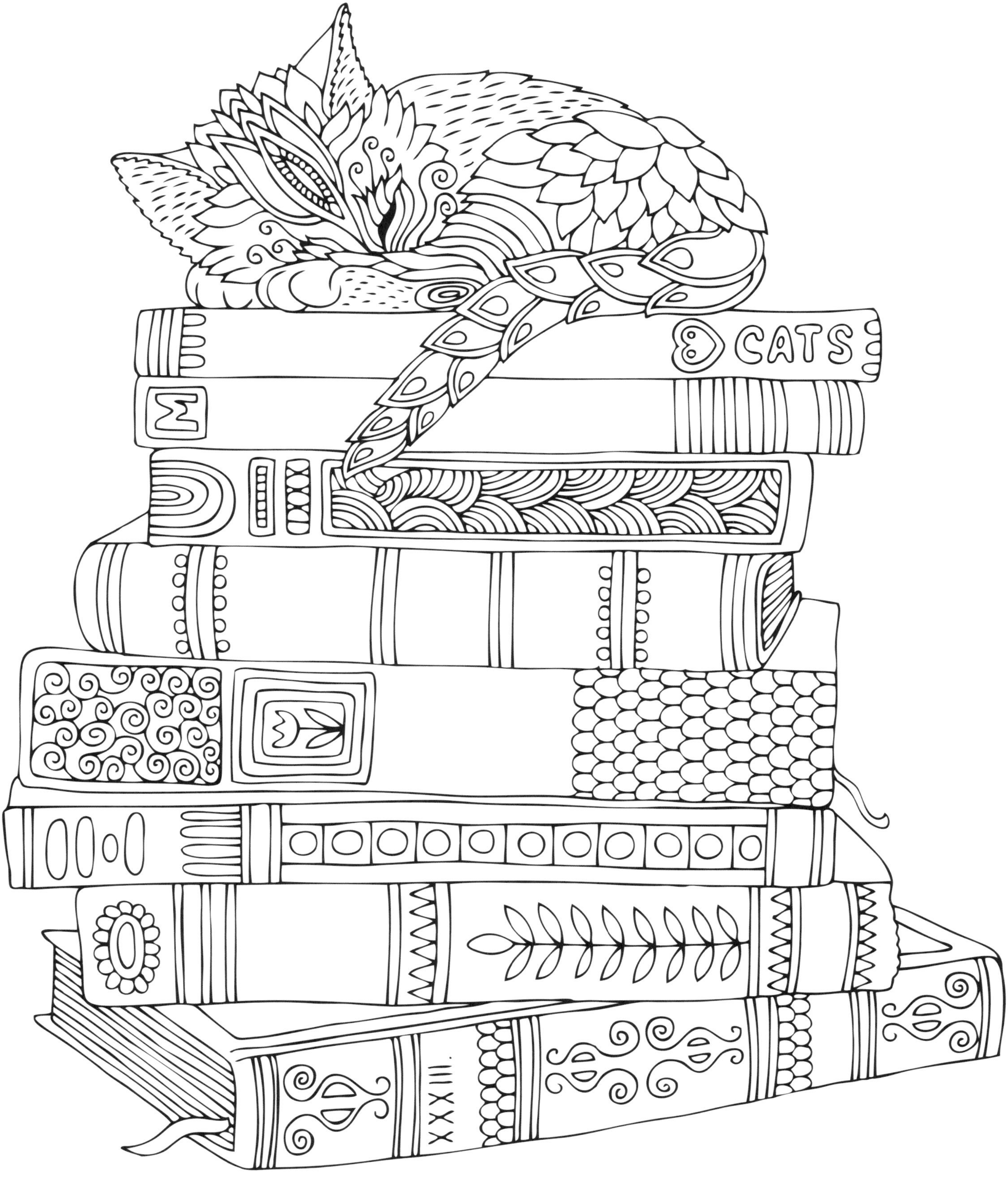
CATS
XXXIII

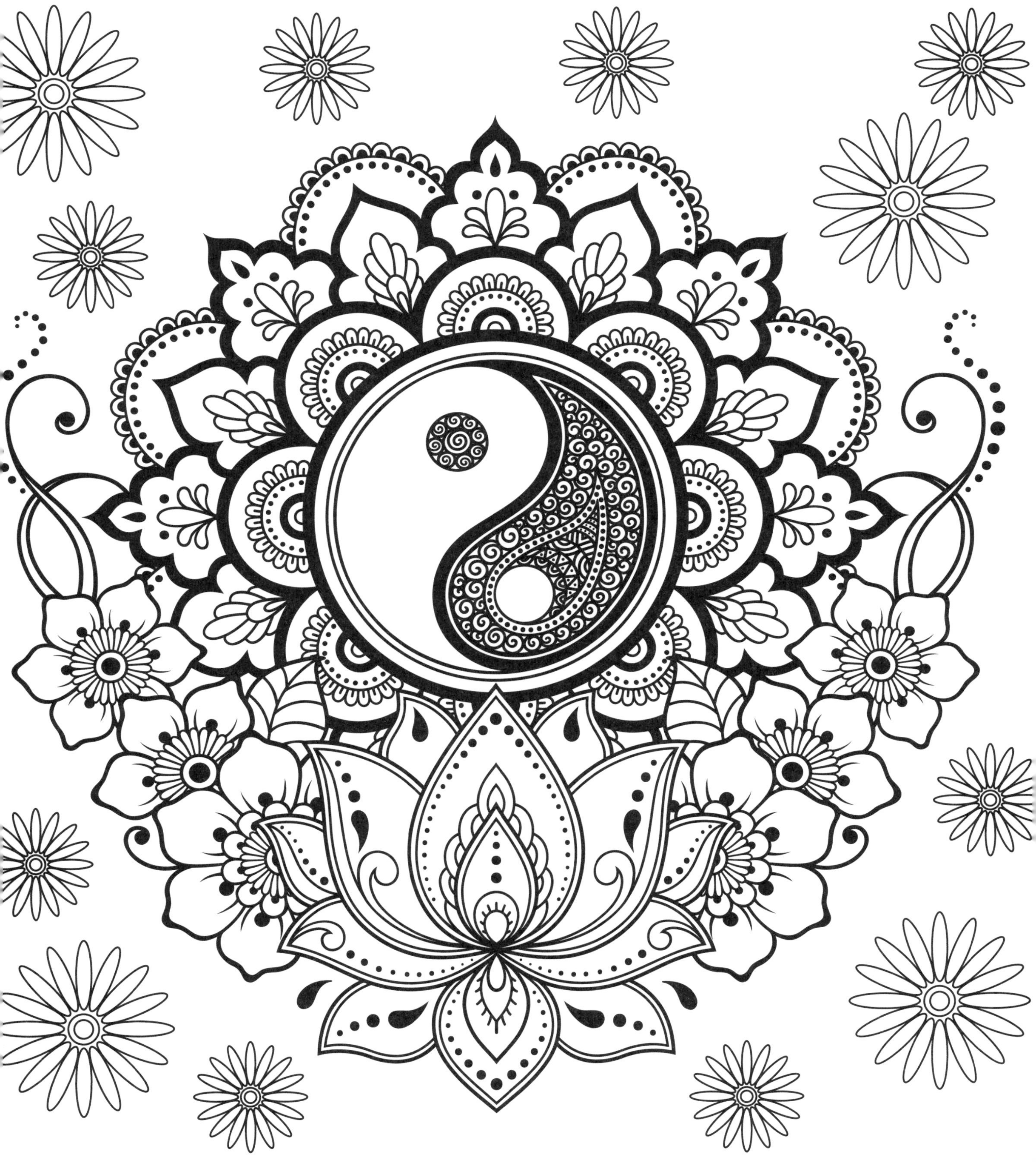

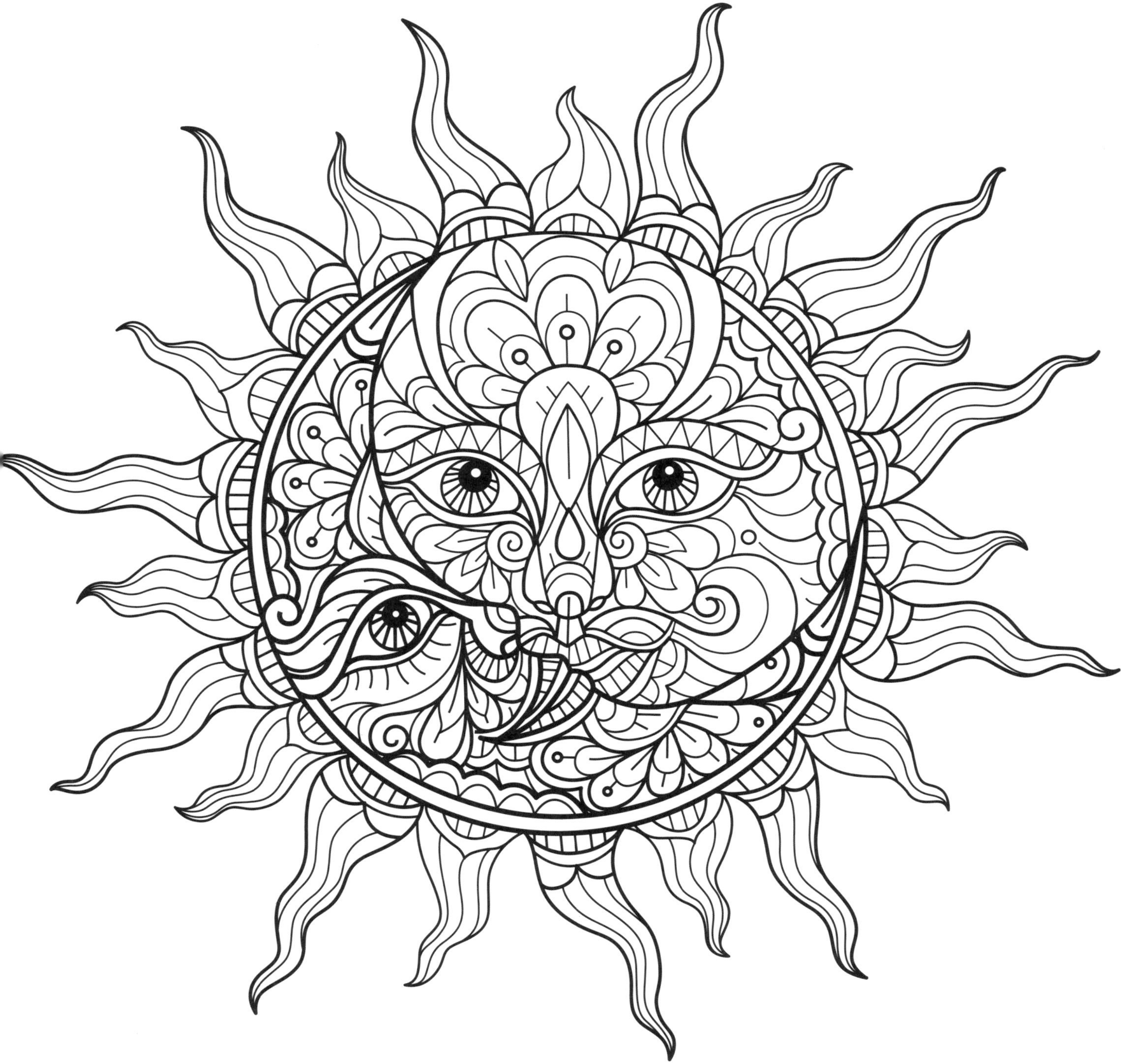

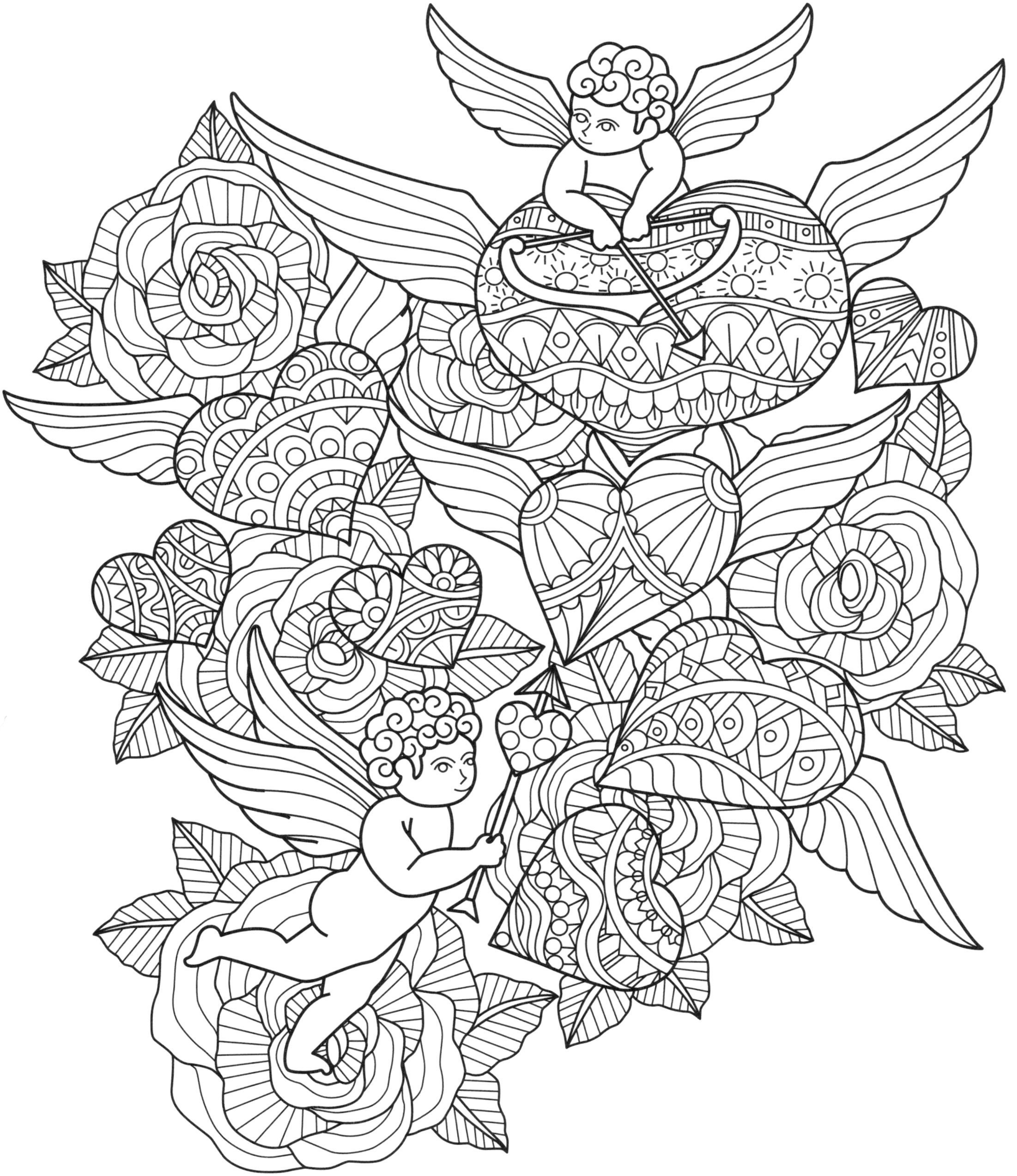

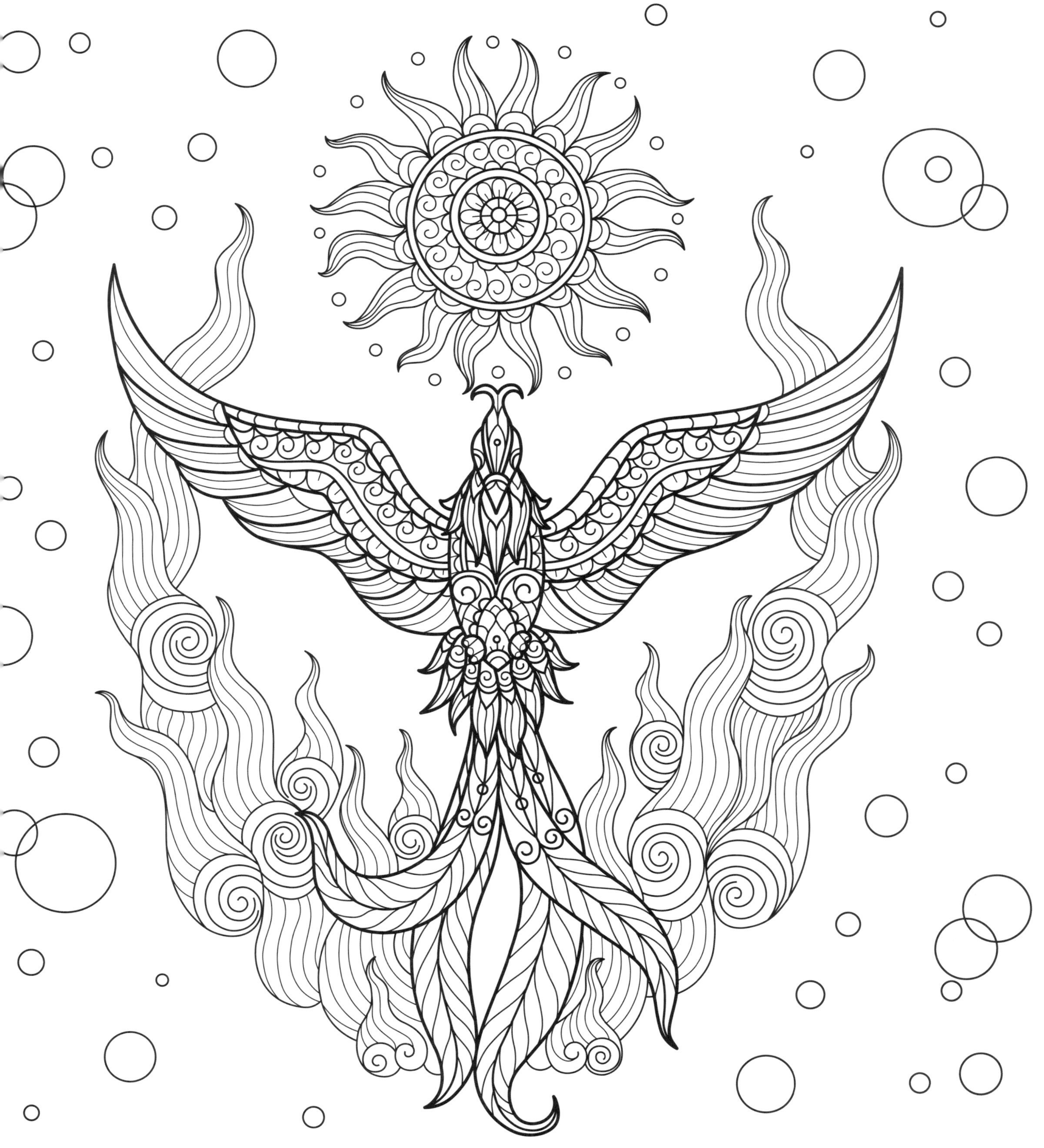

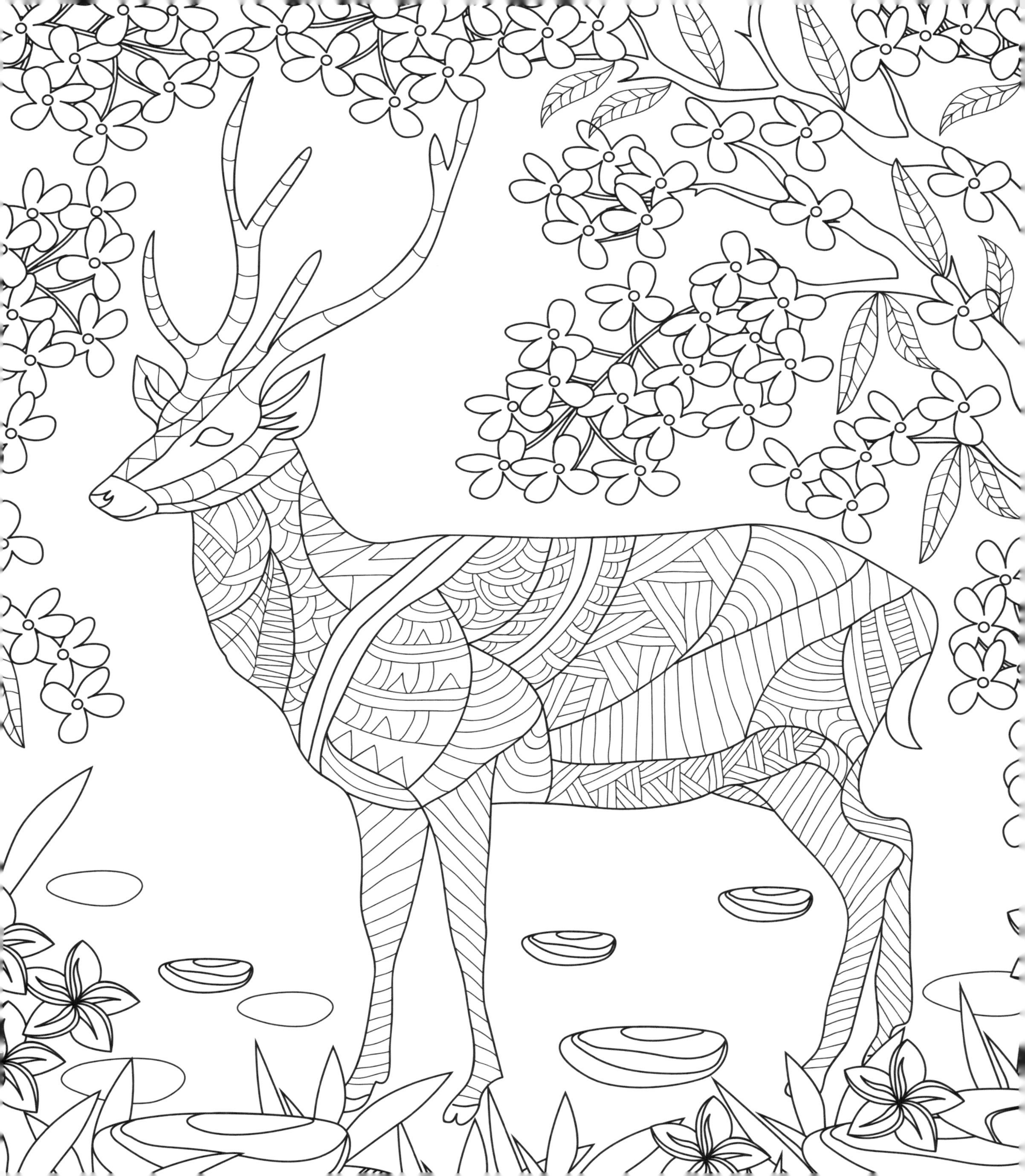

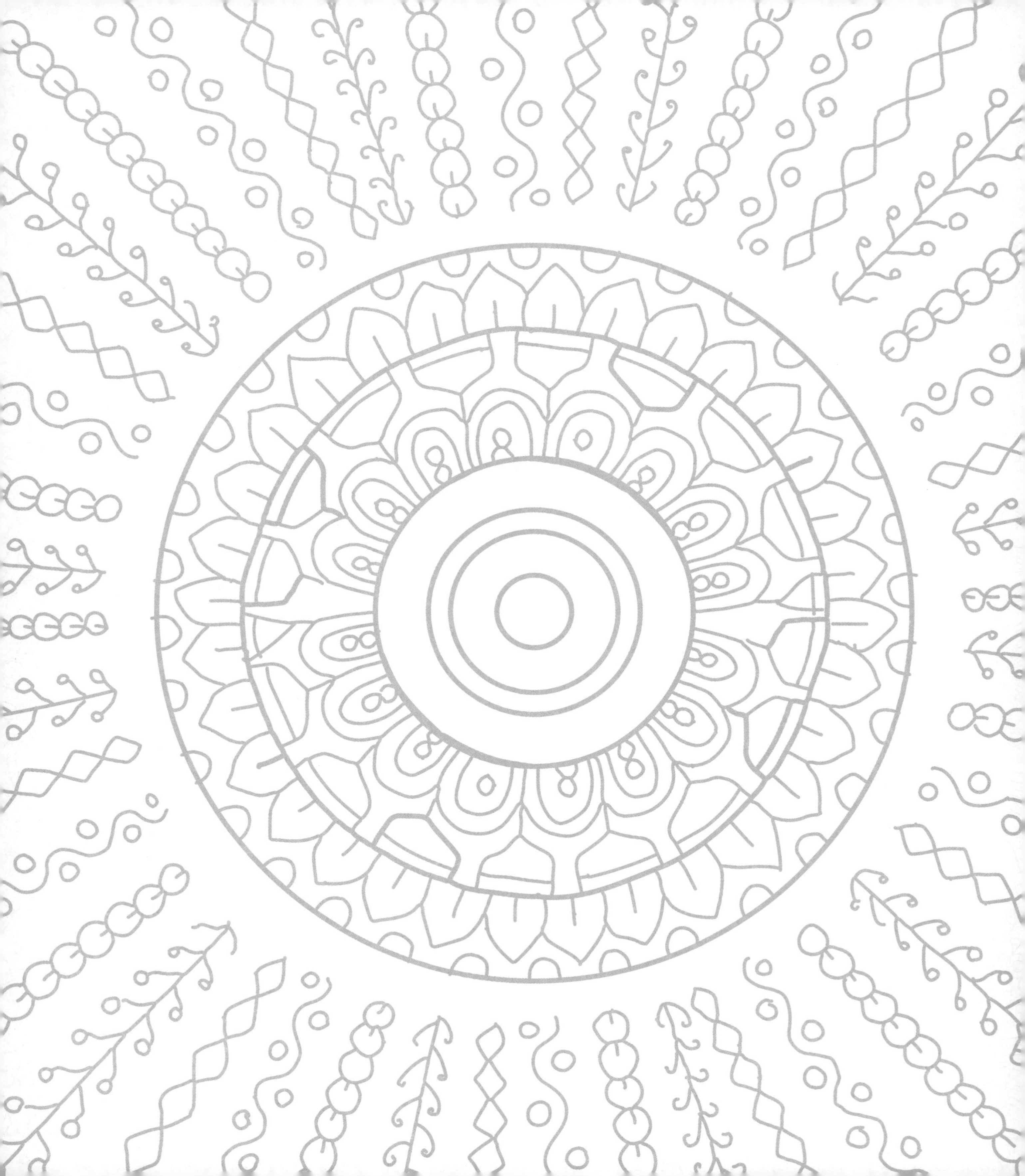

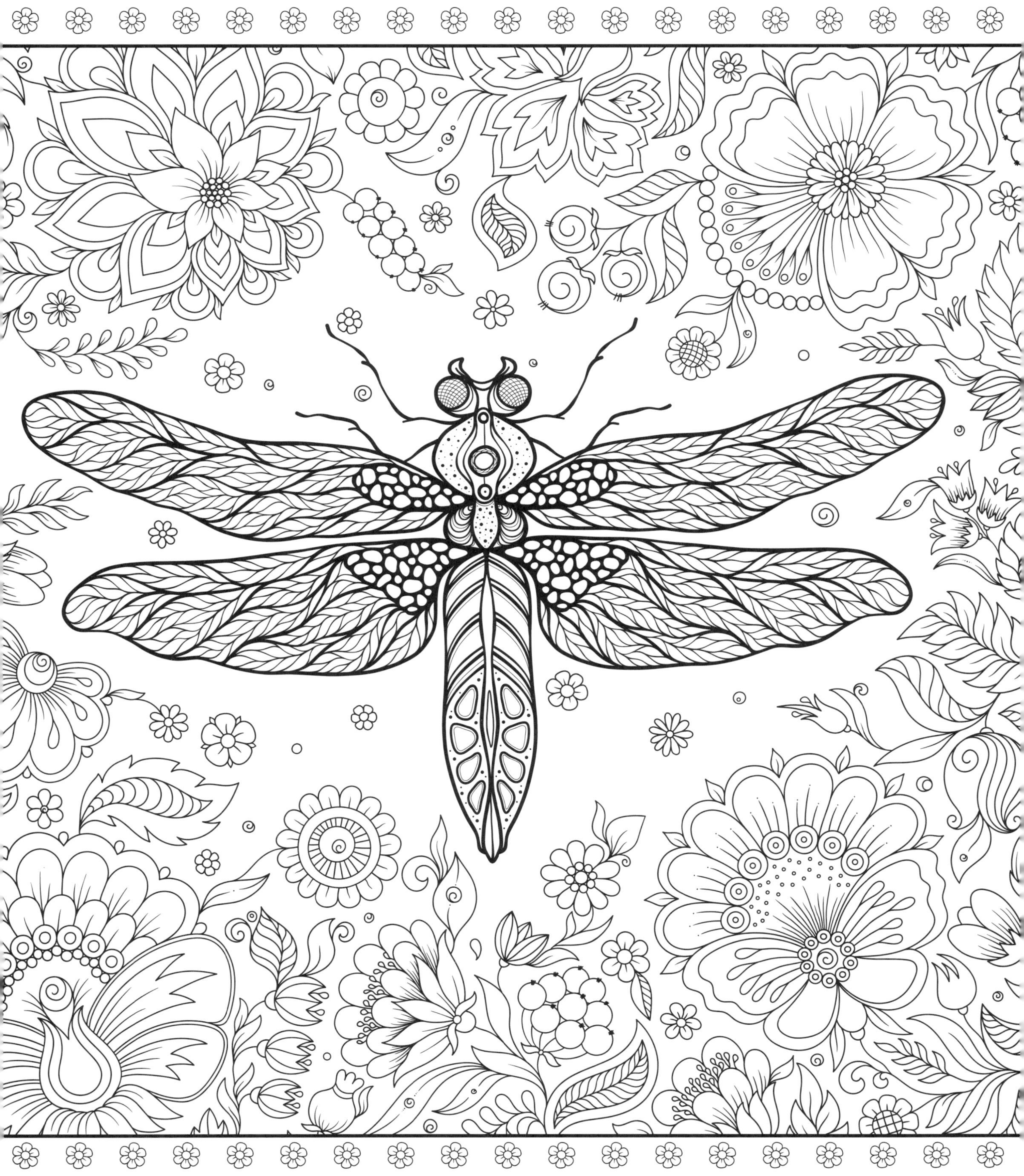

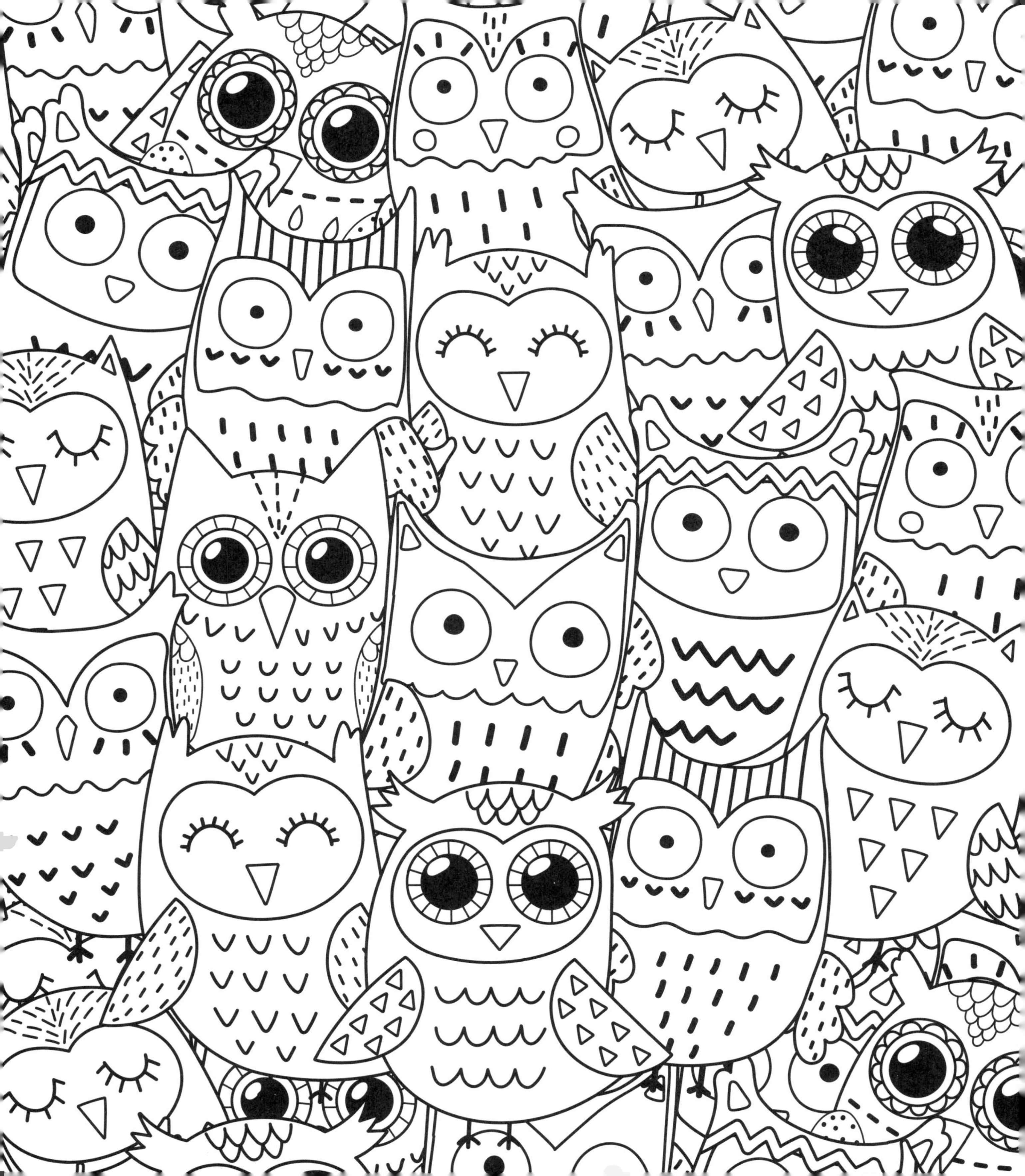

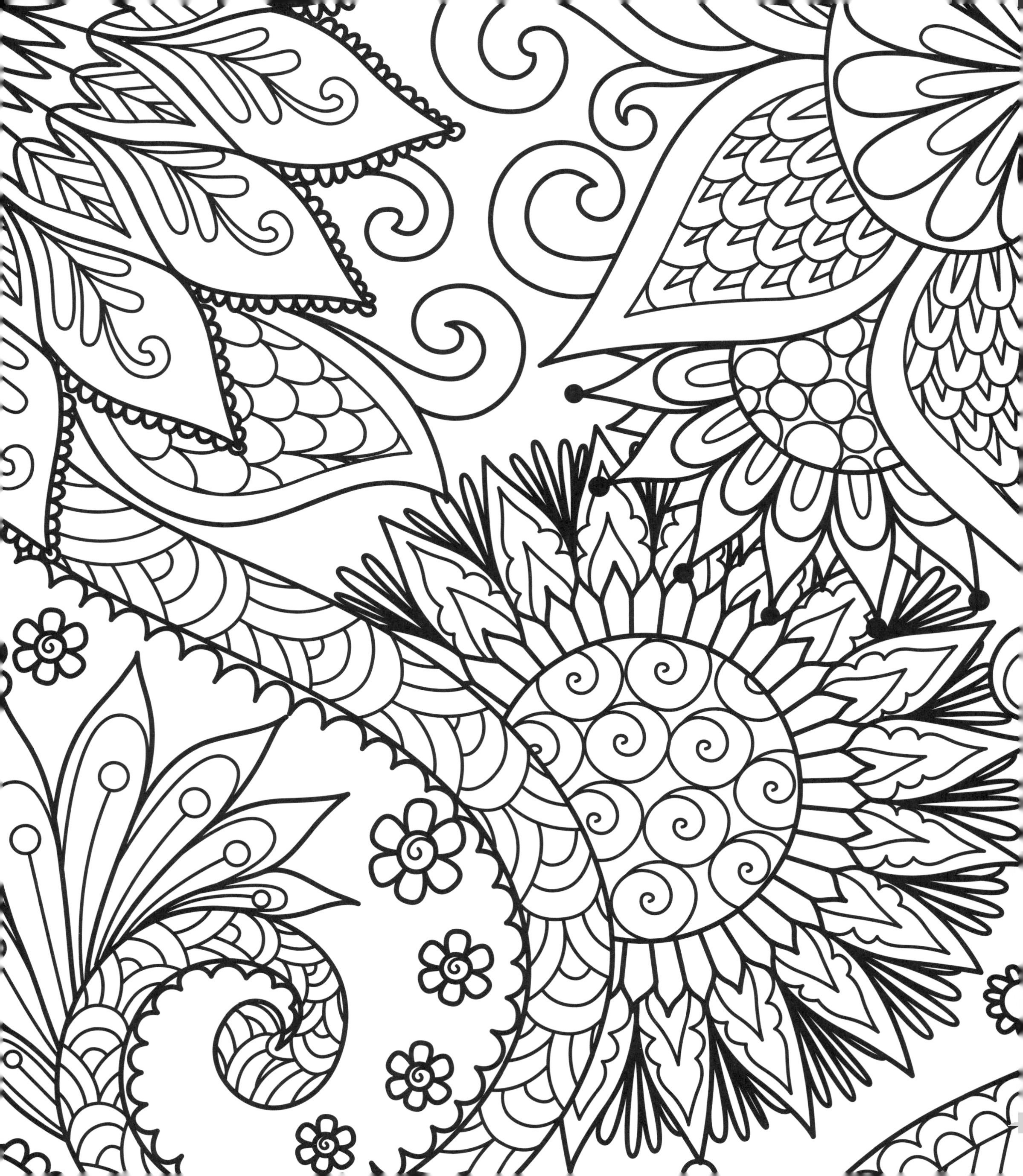

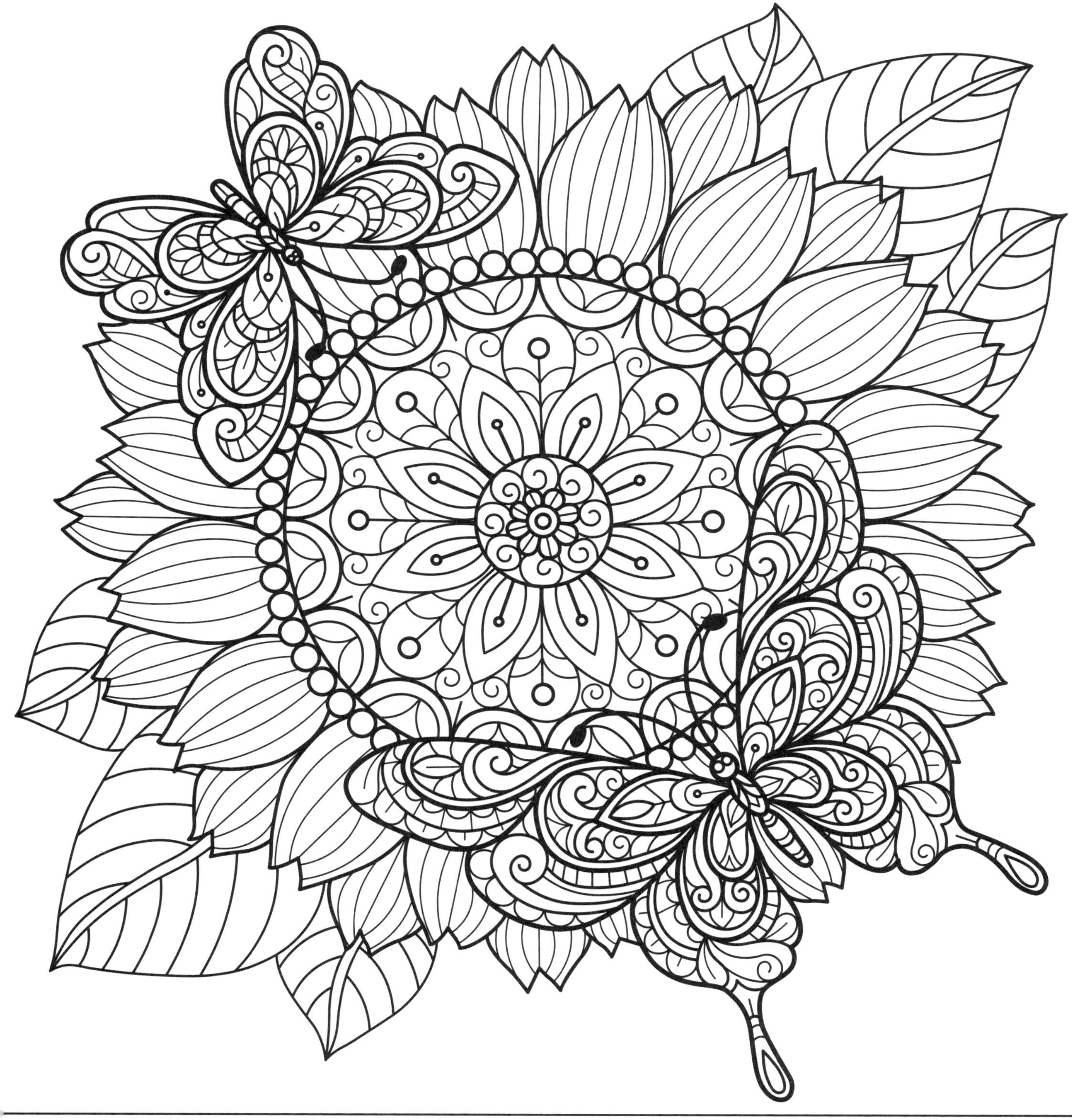

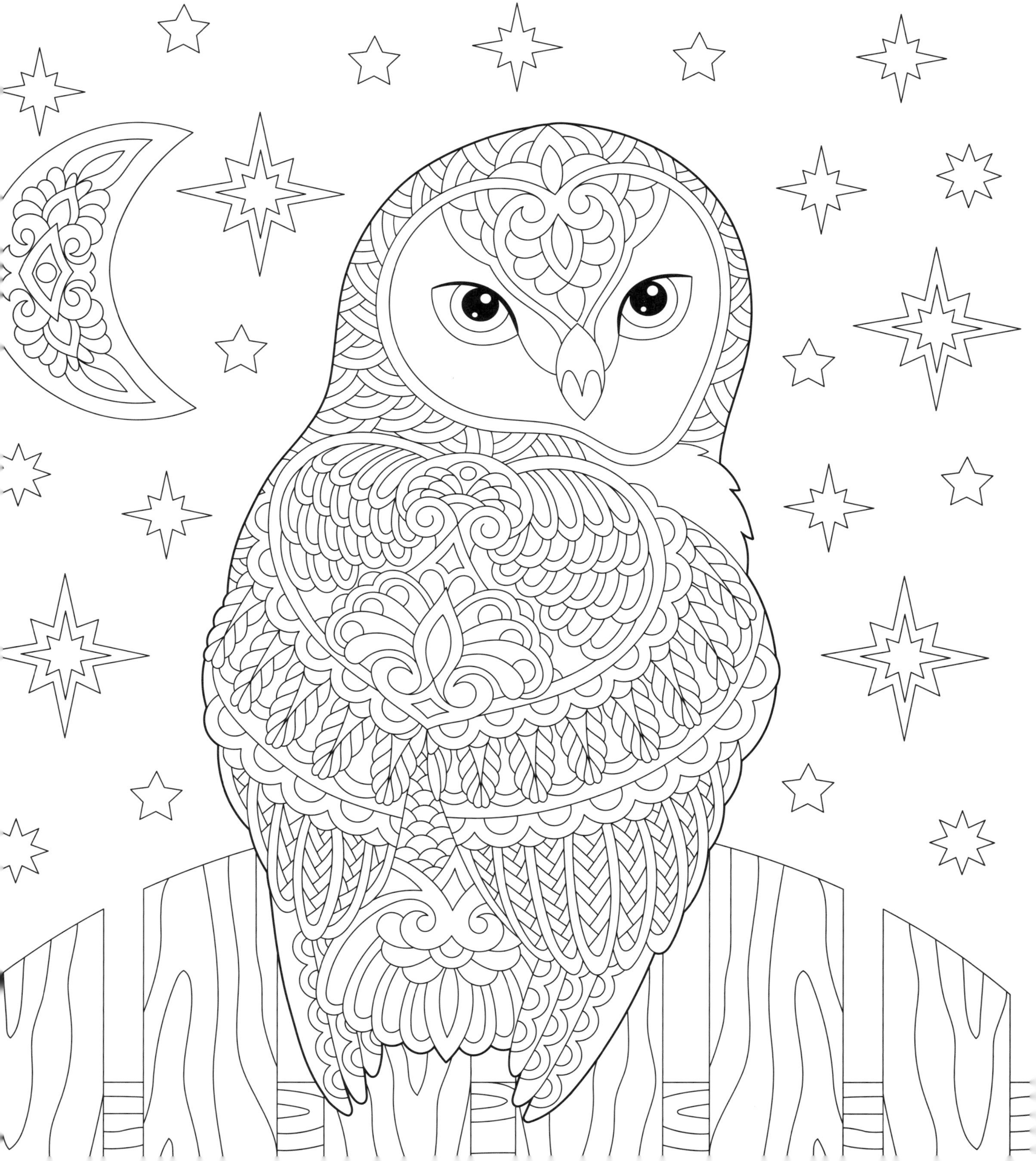

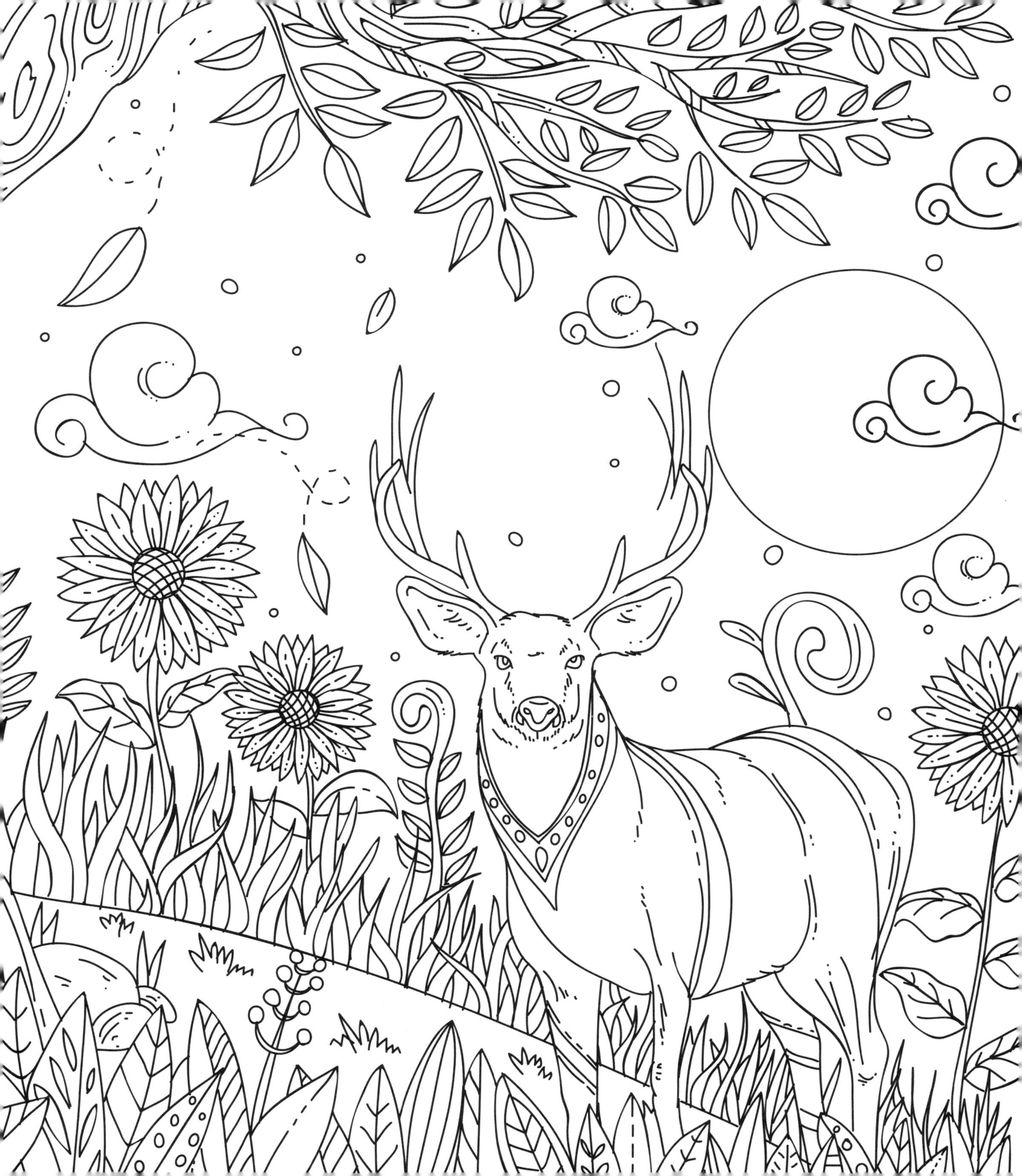

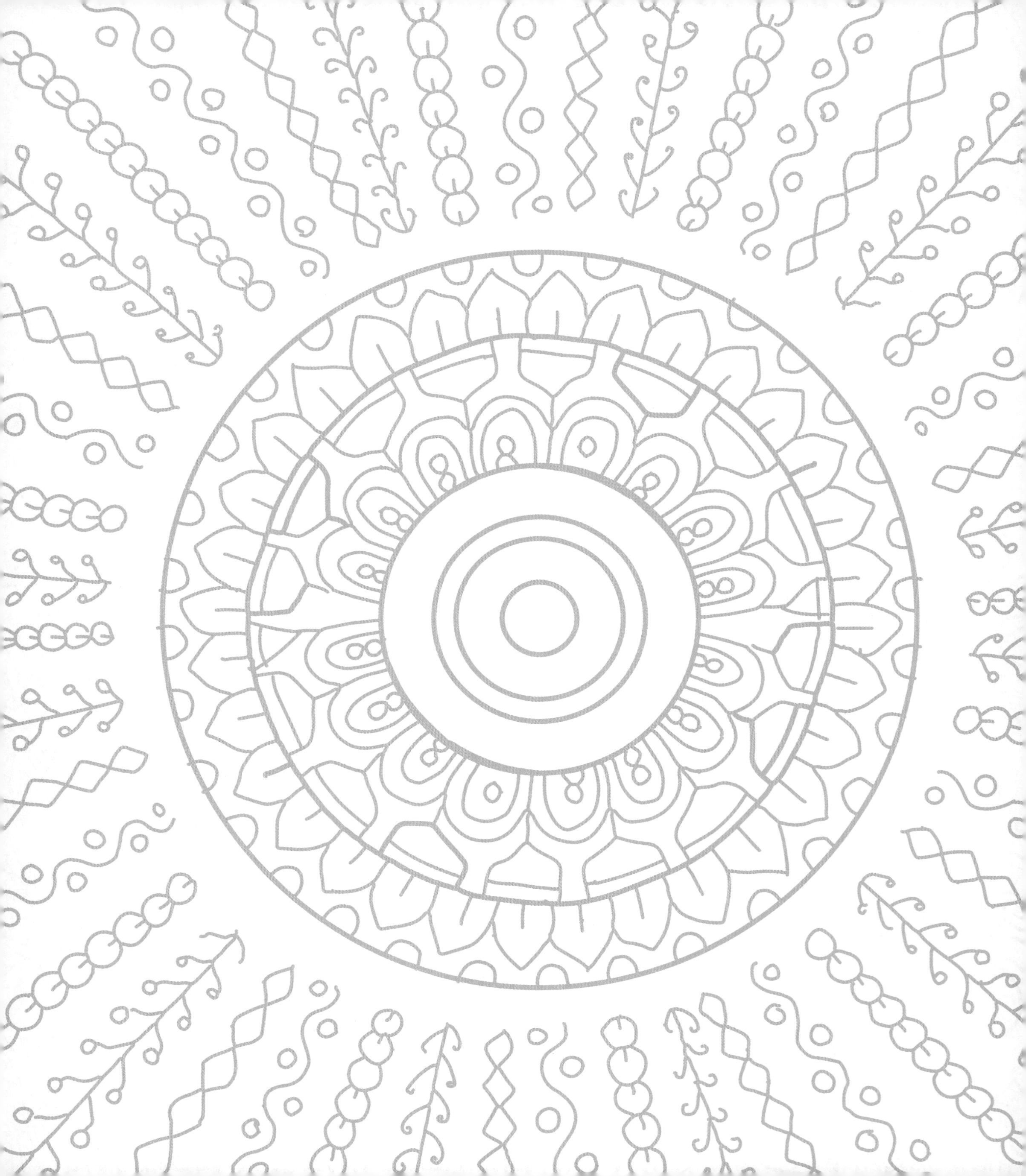

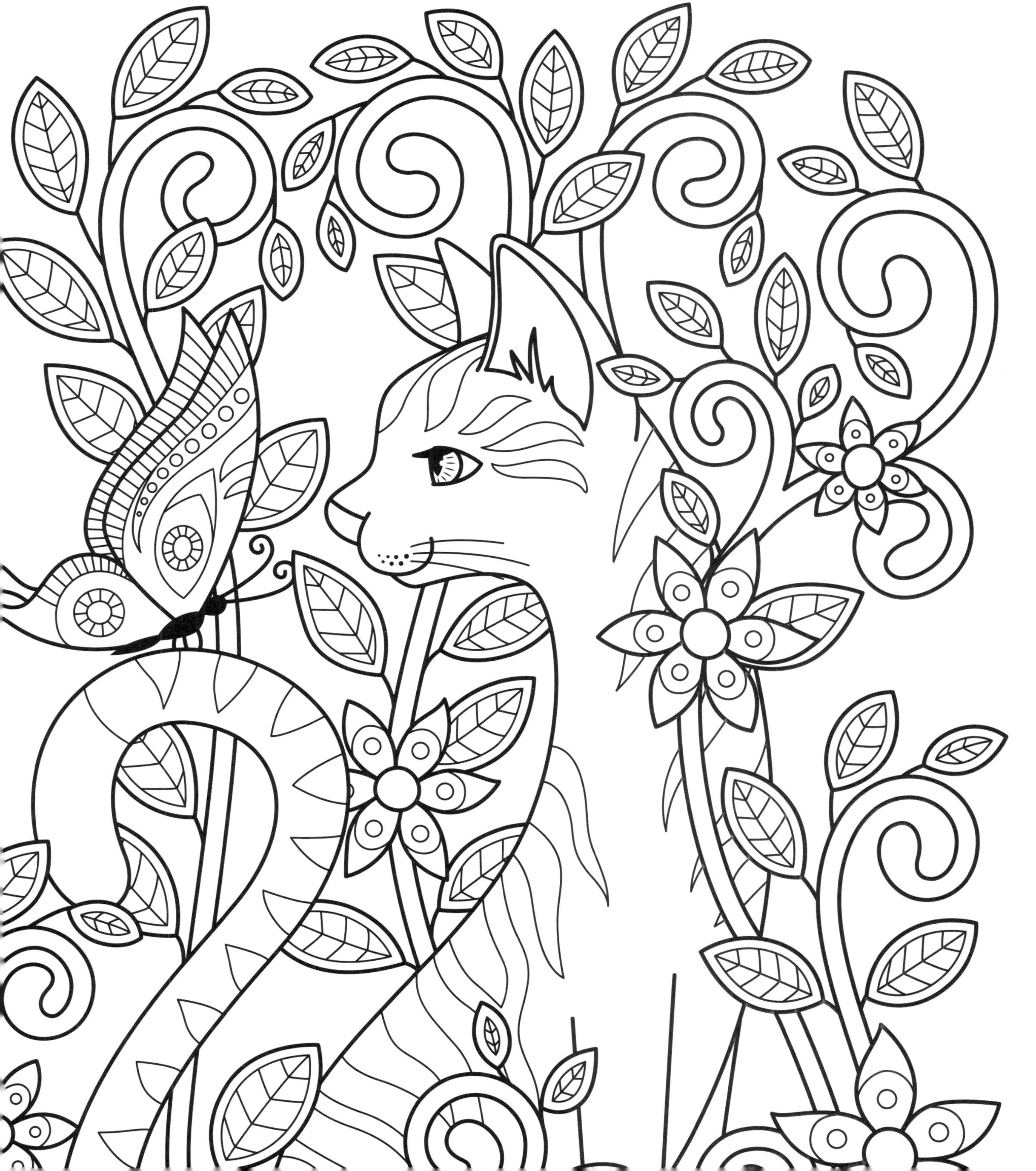

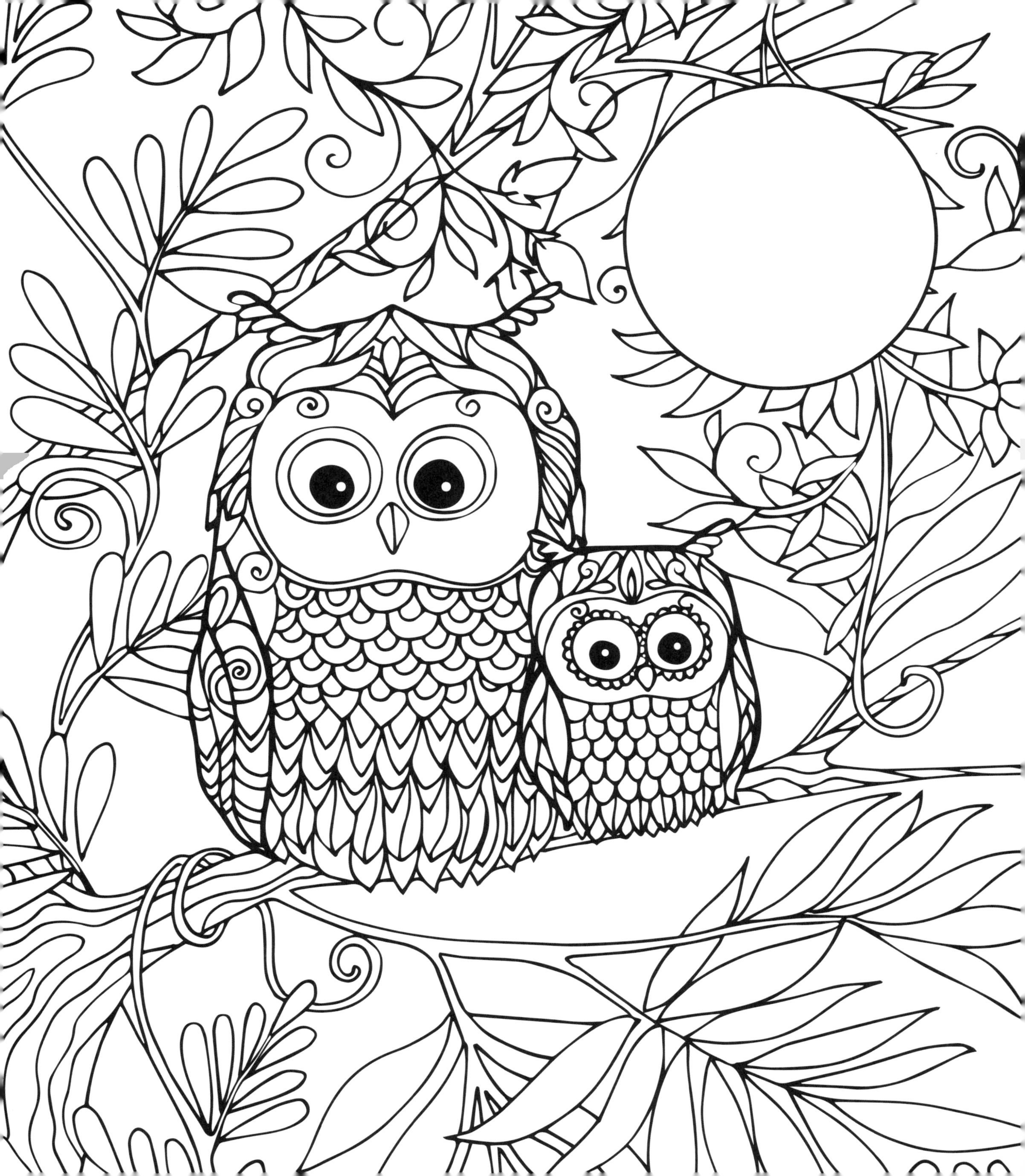

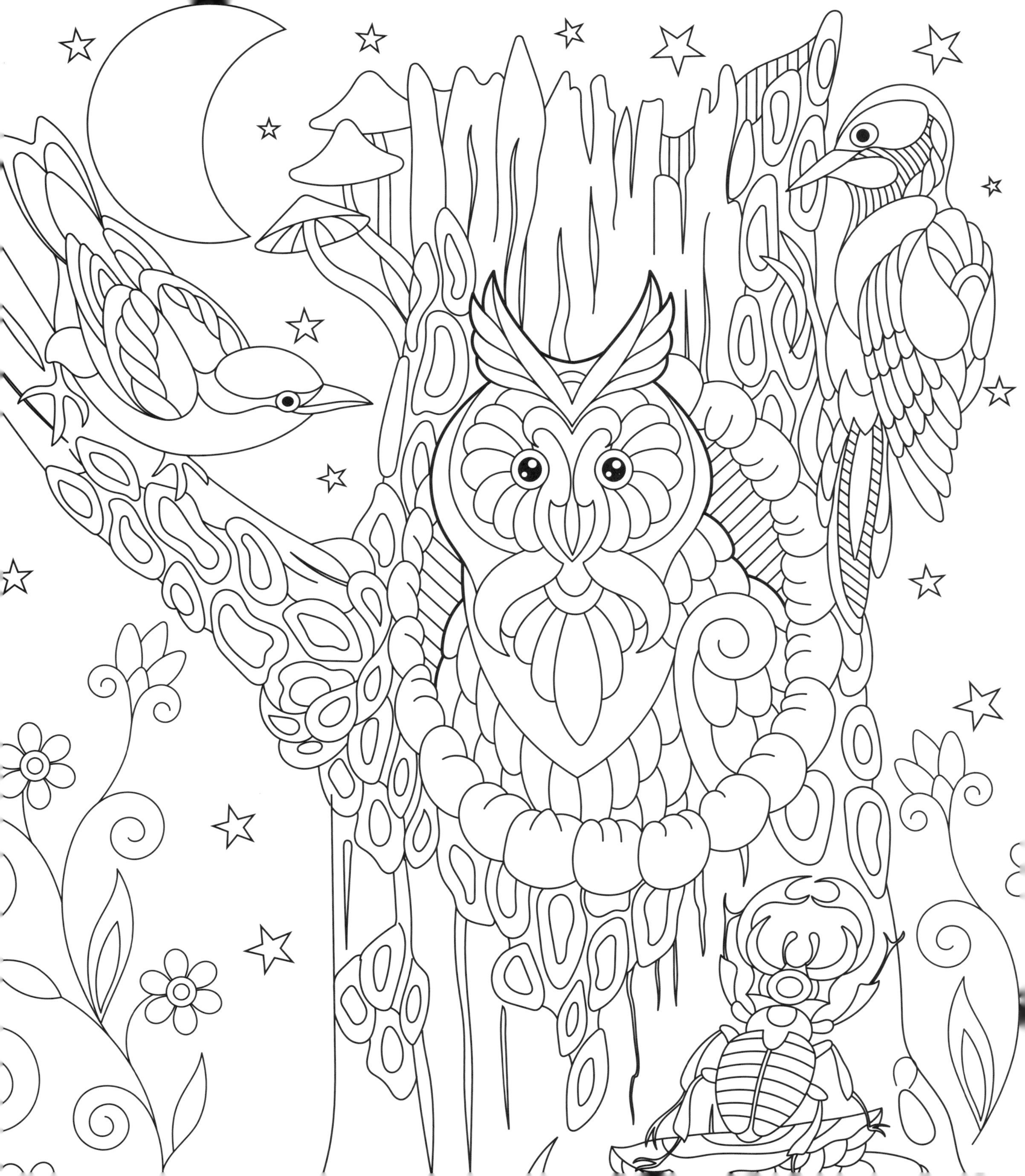

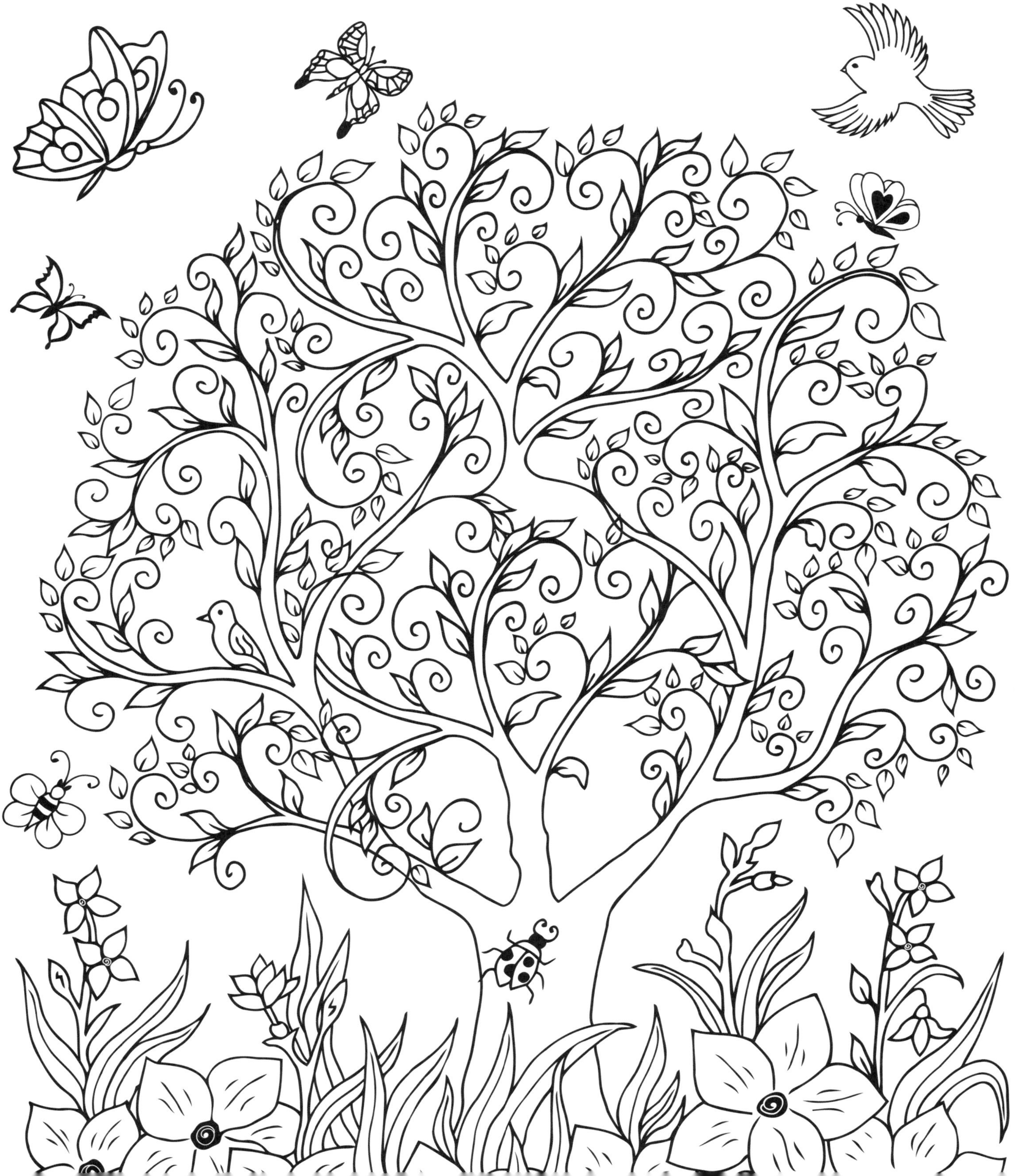

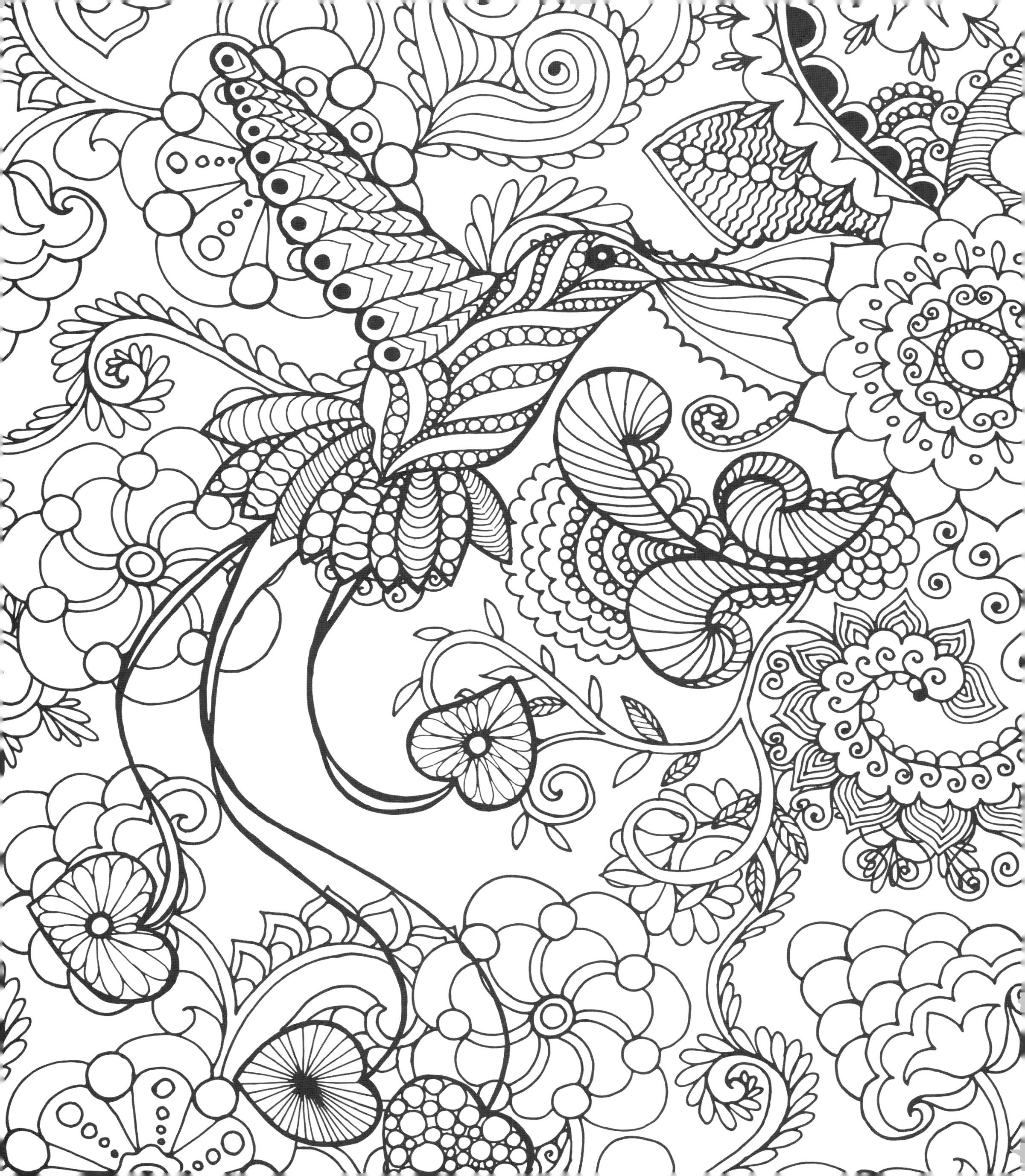

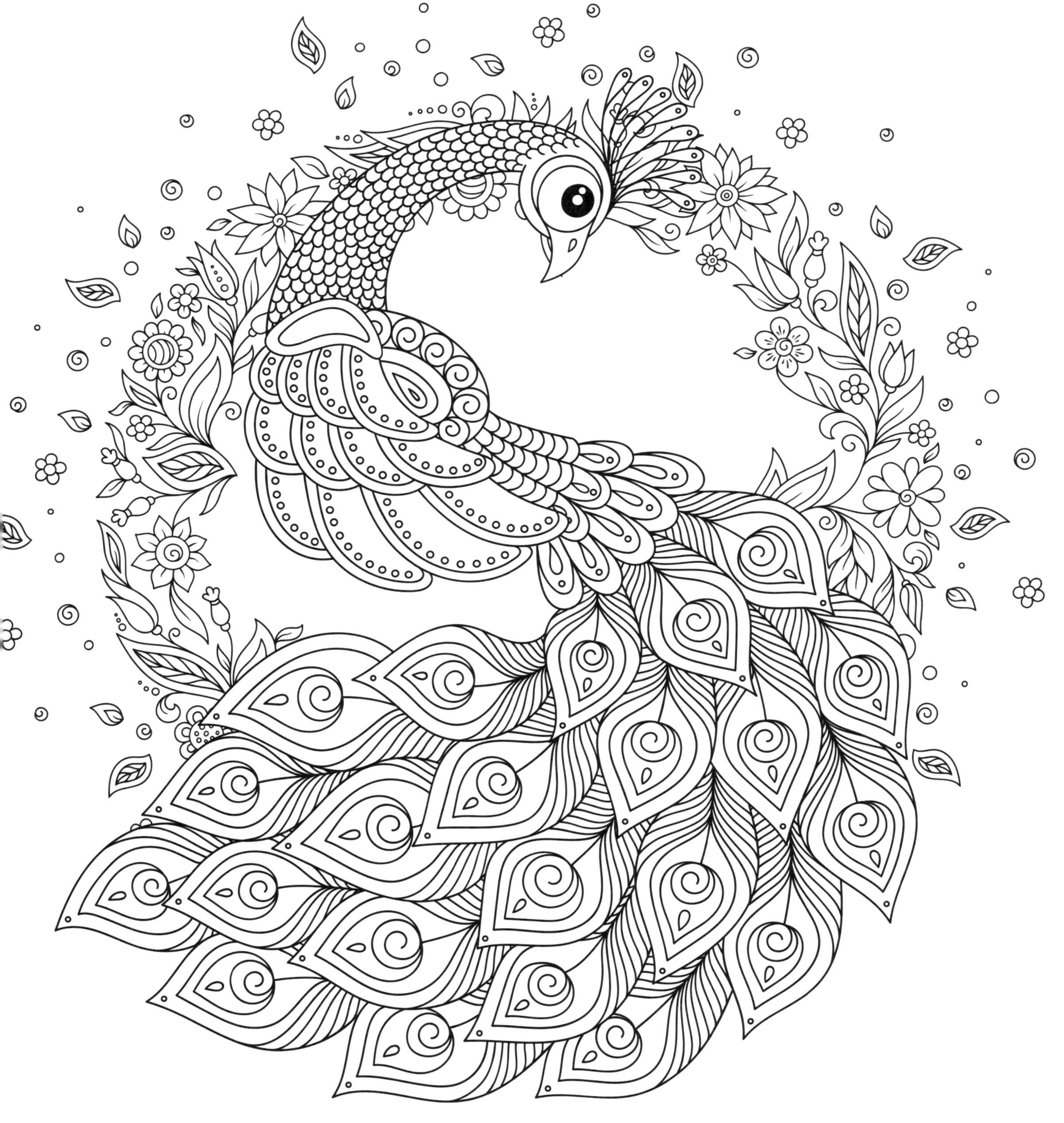

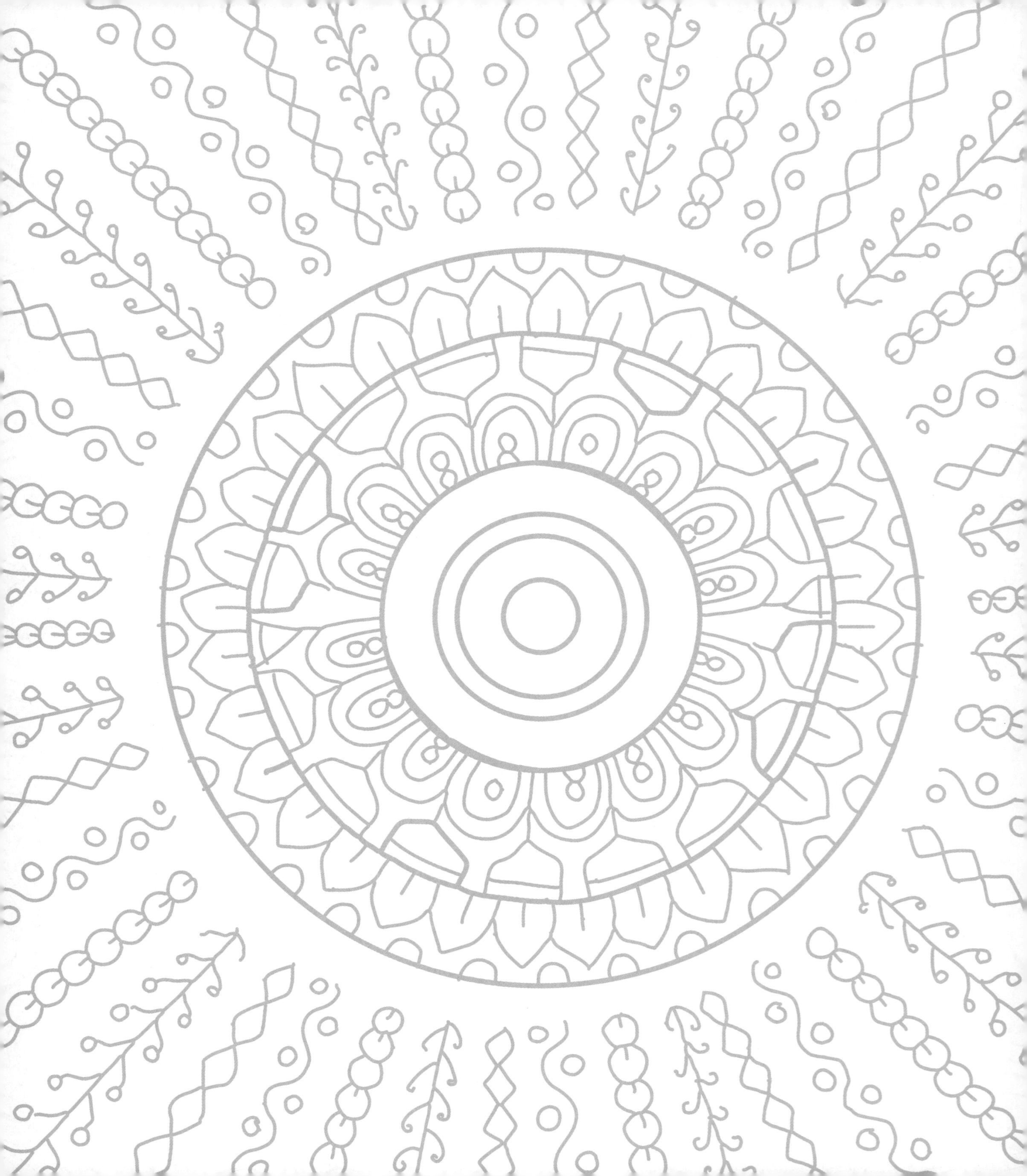

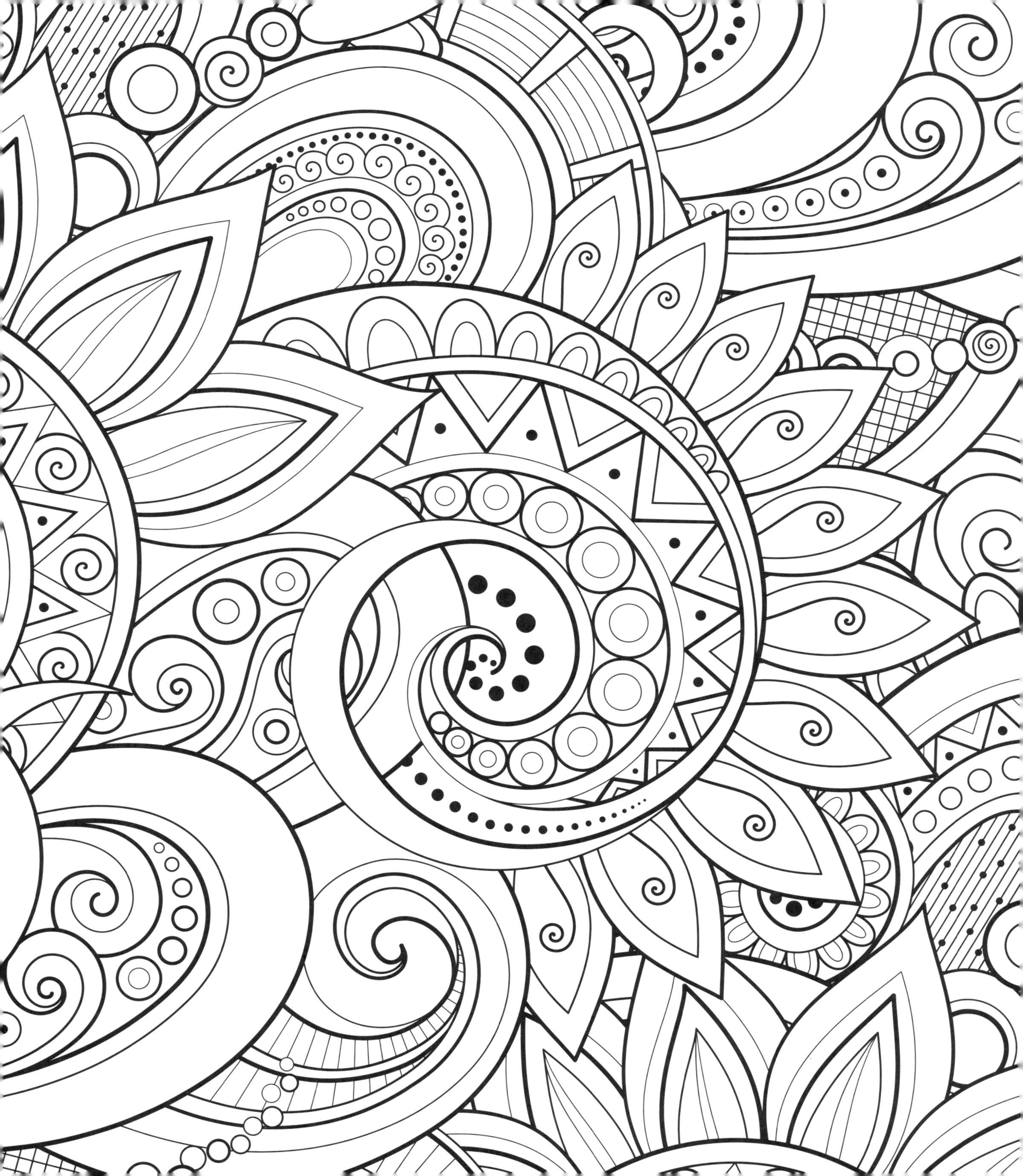

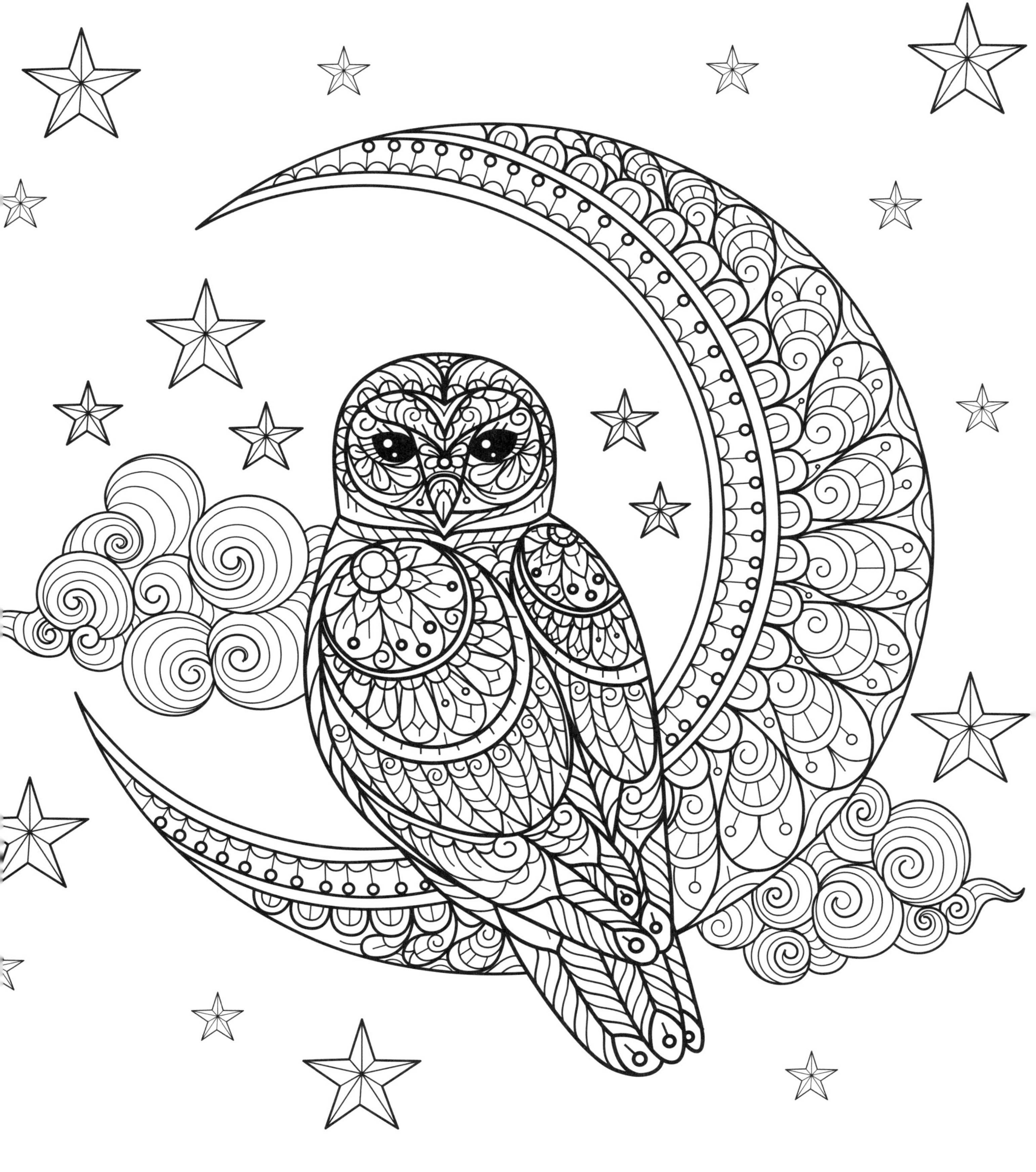

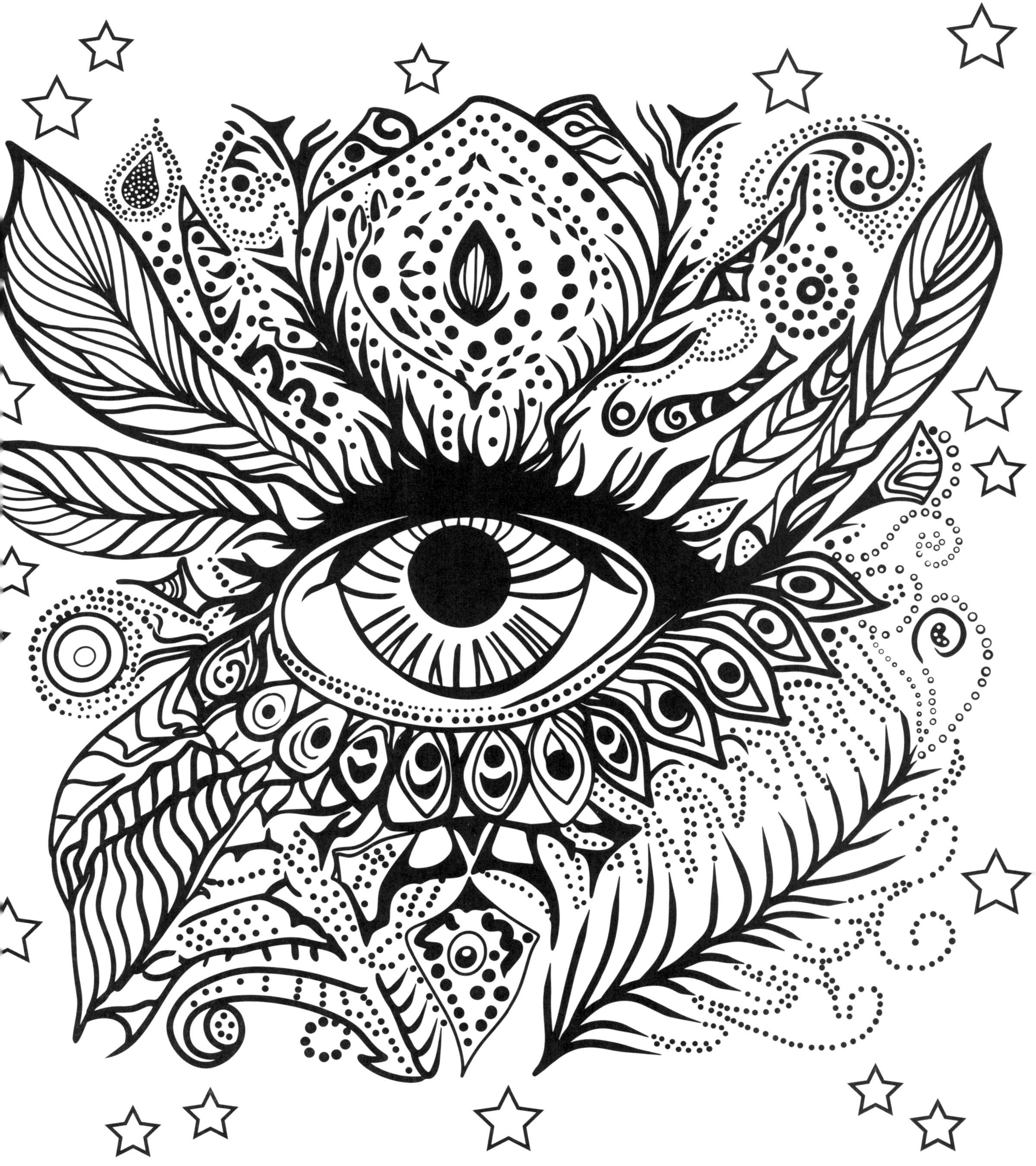

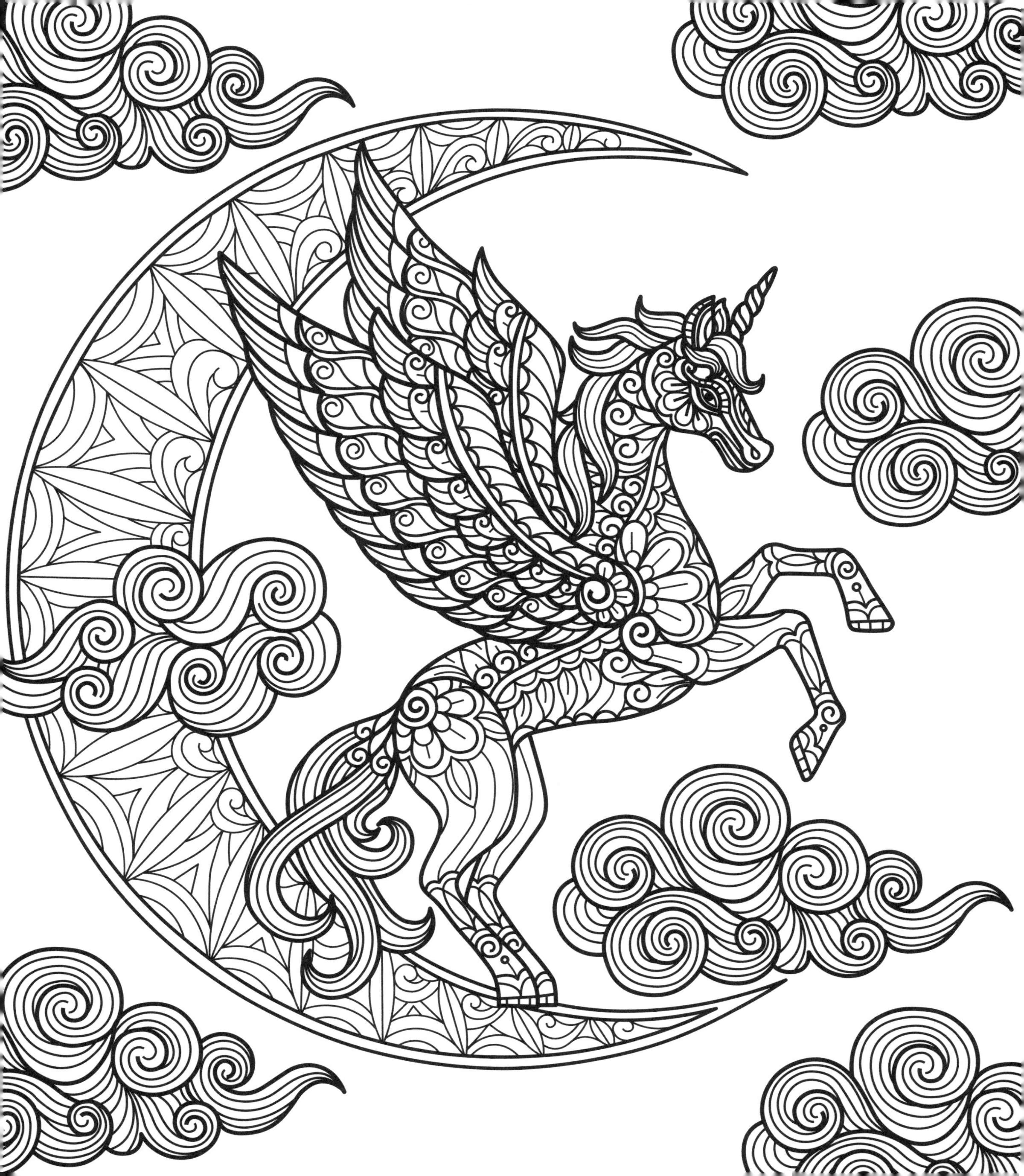

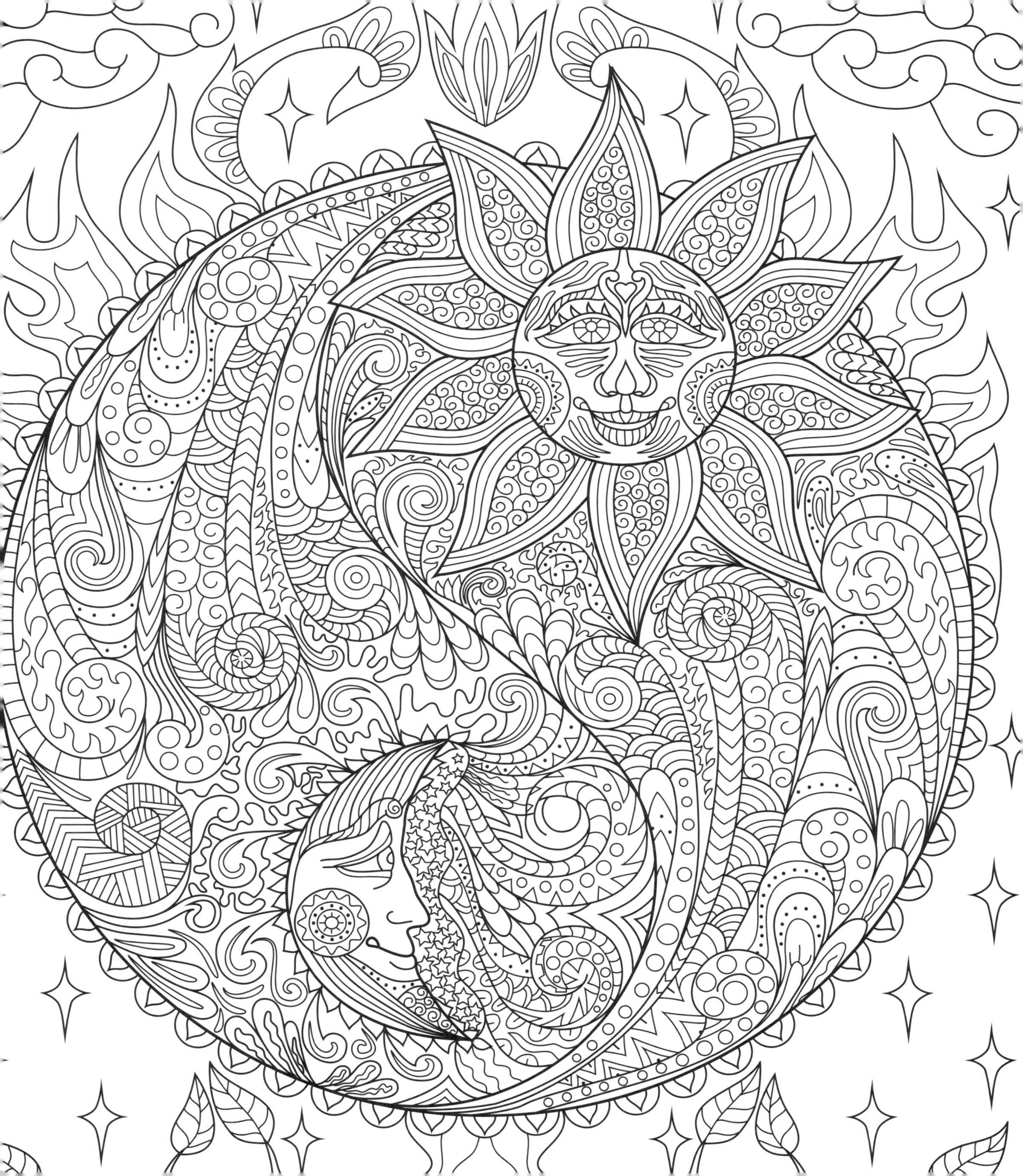

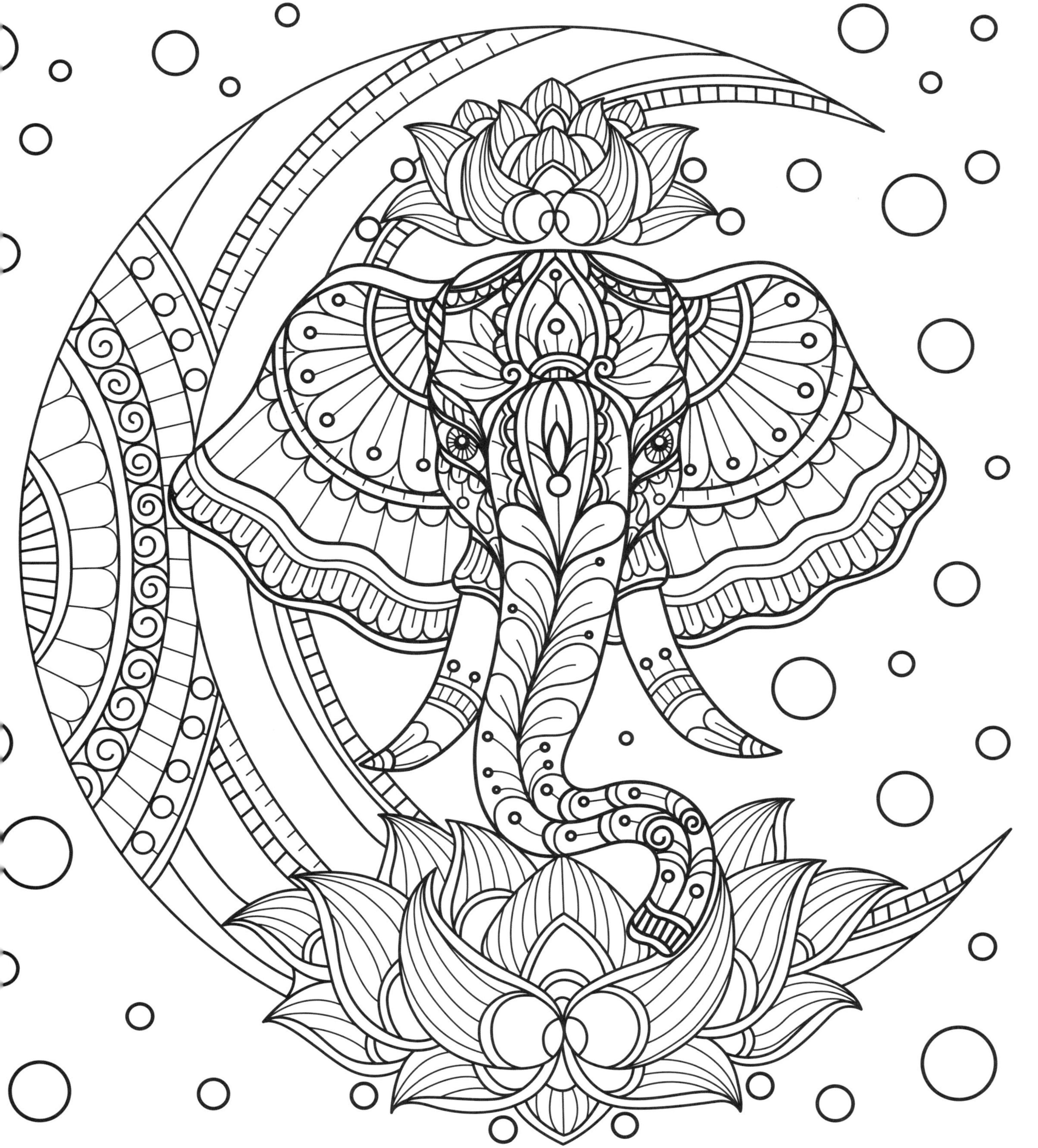

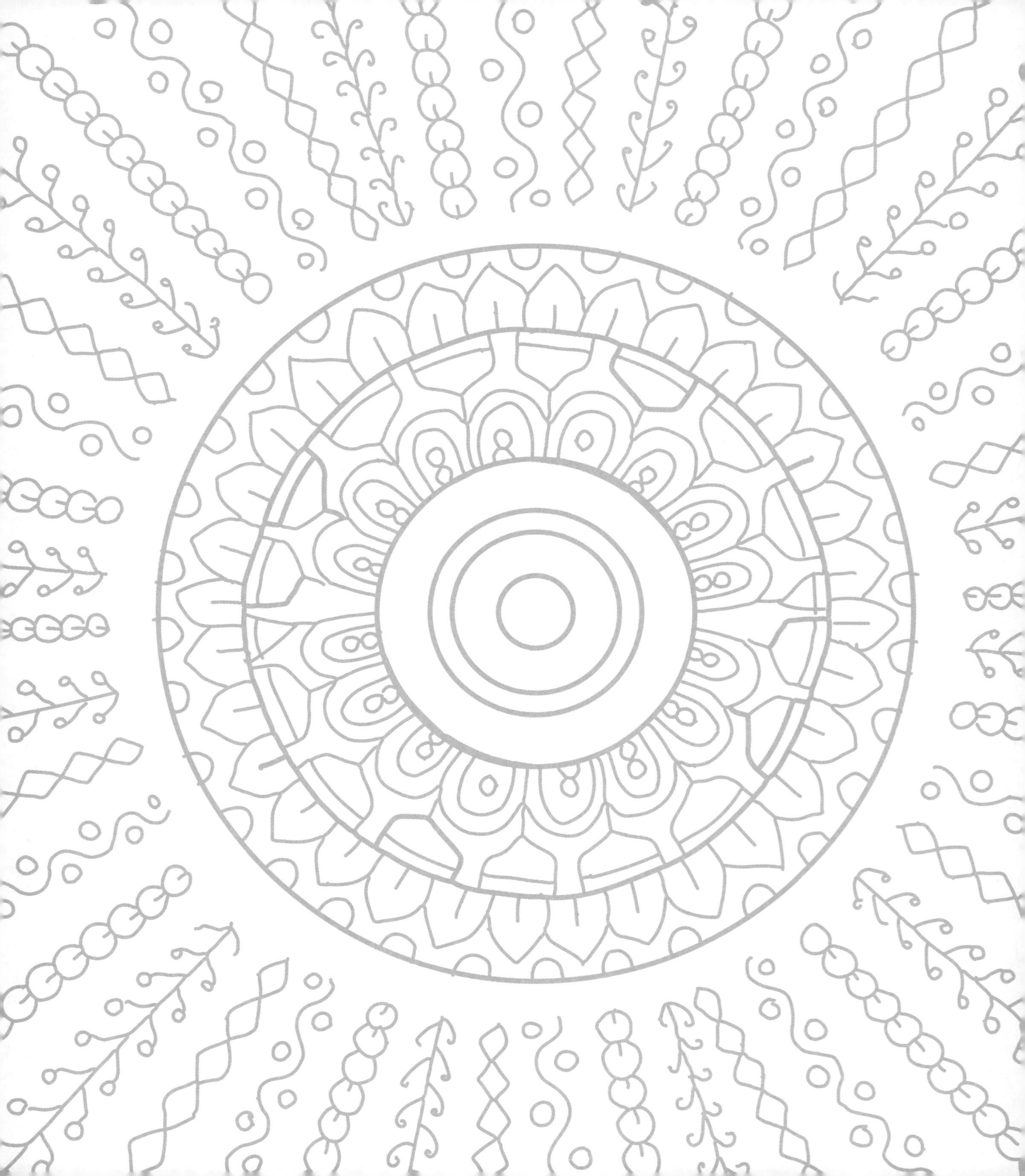

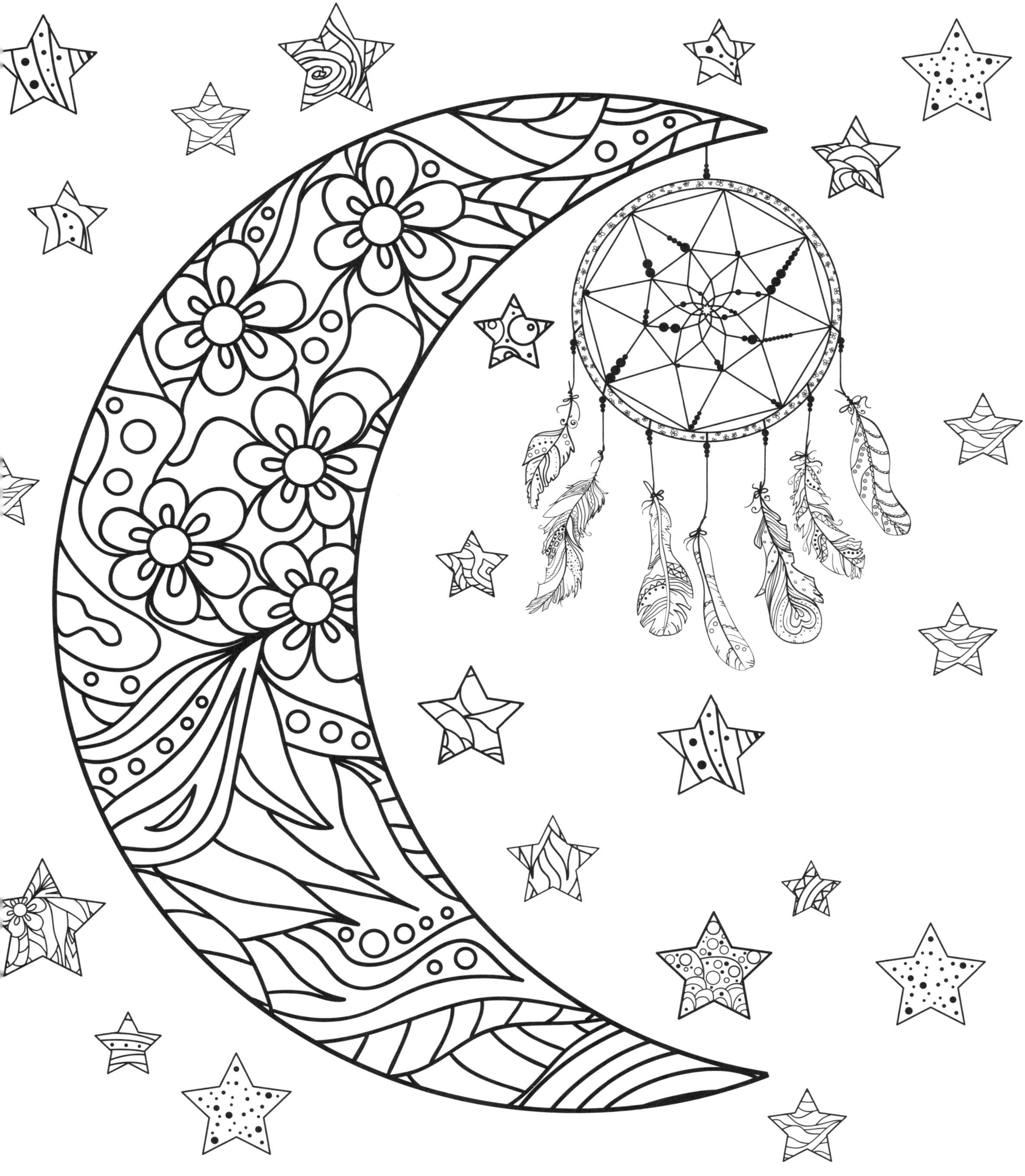

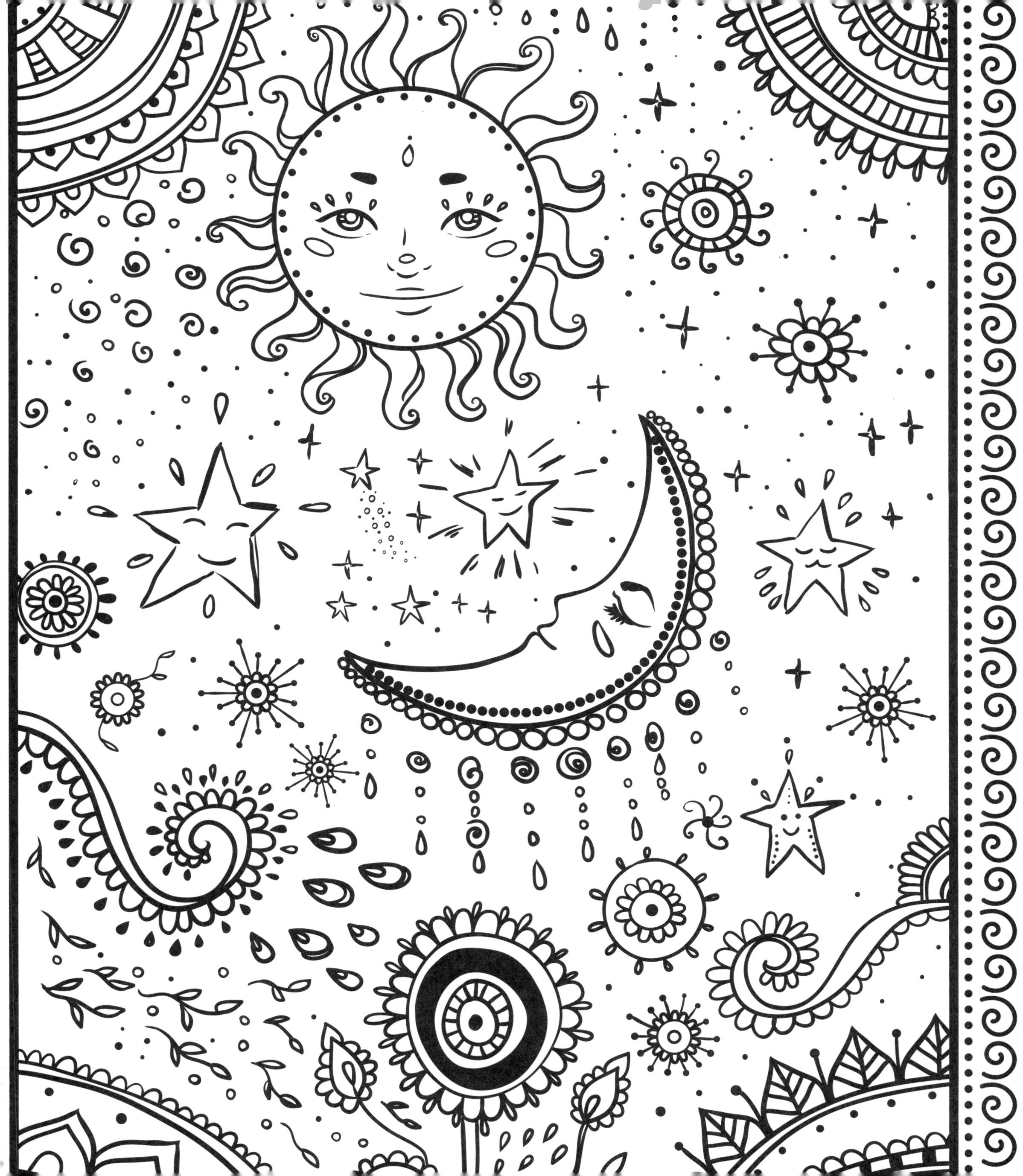

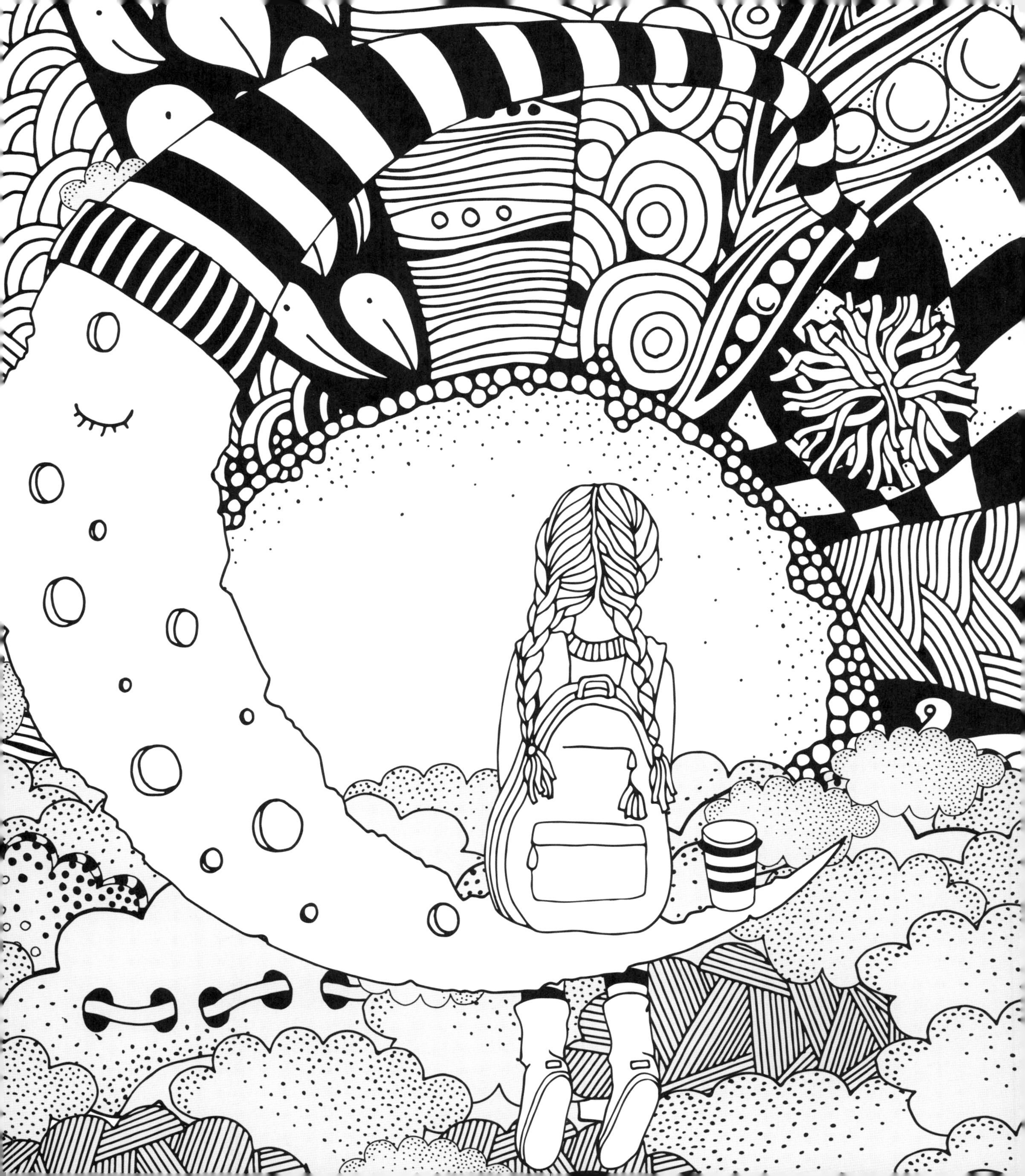

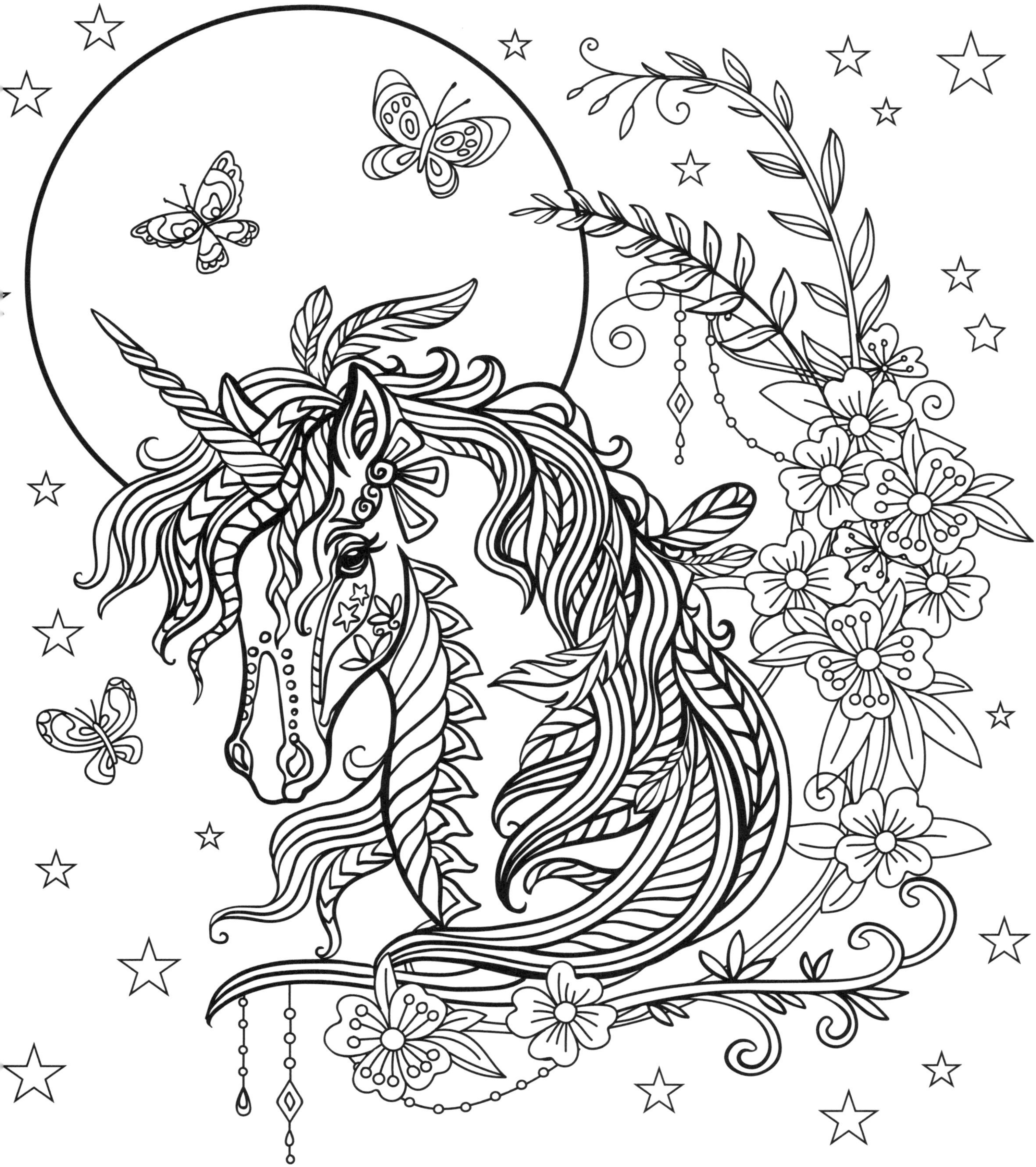

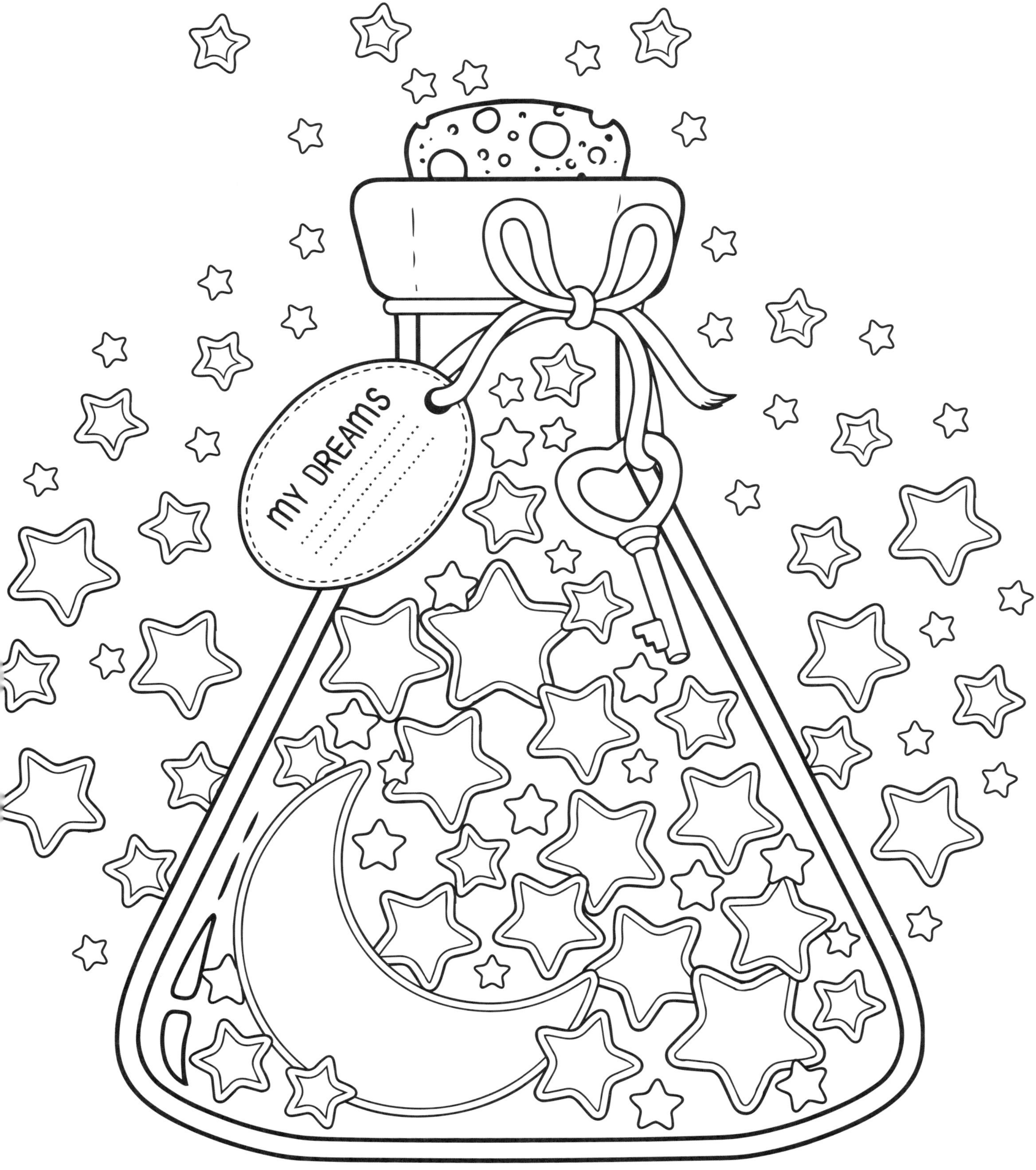
MY DREAMS

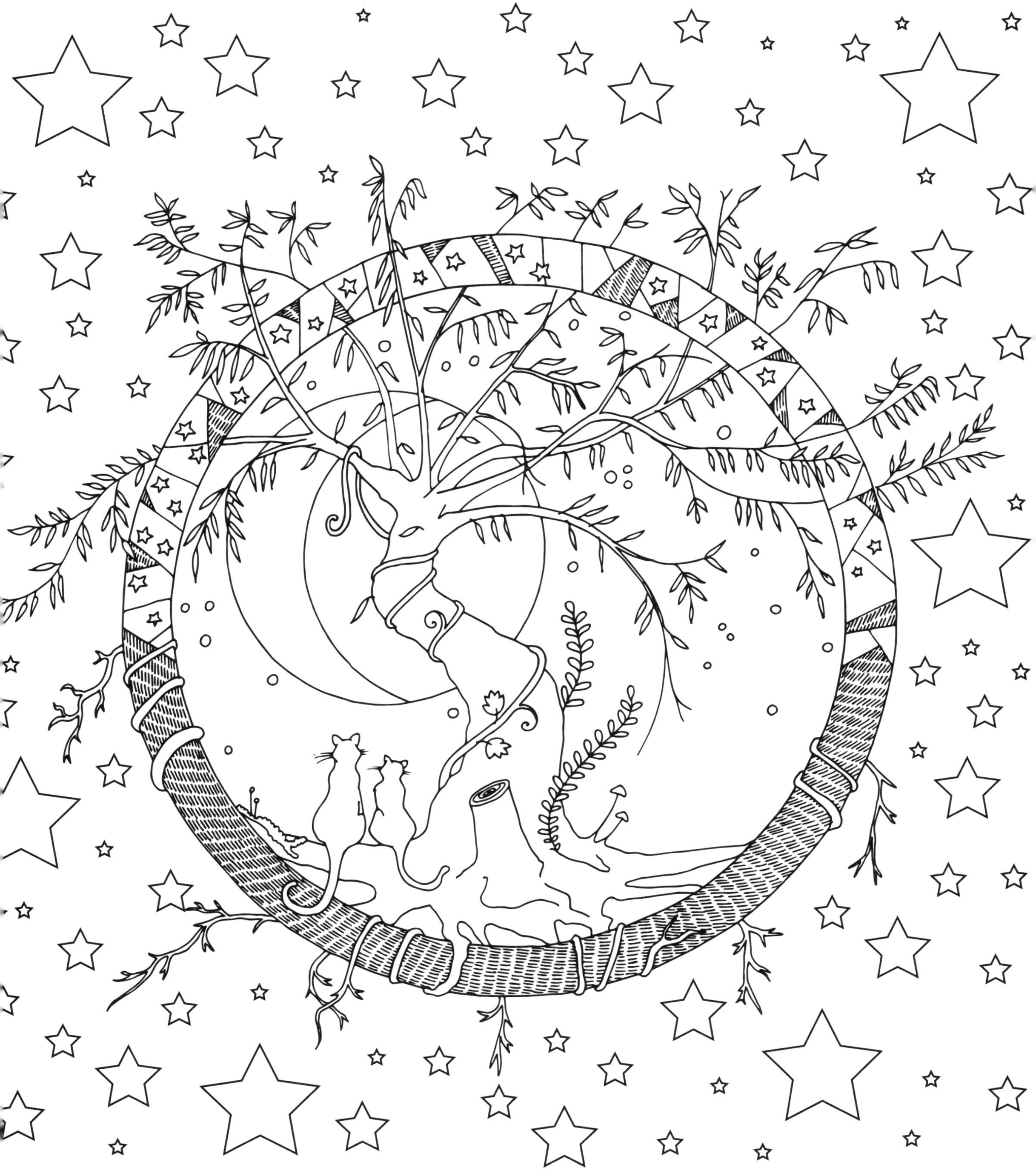

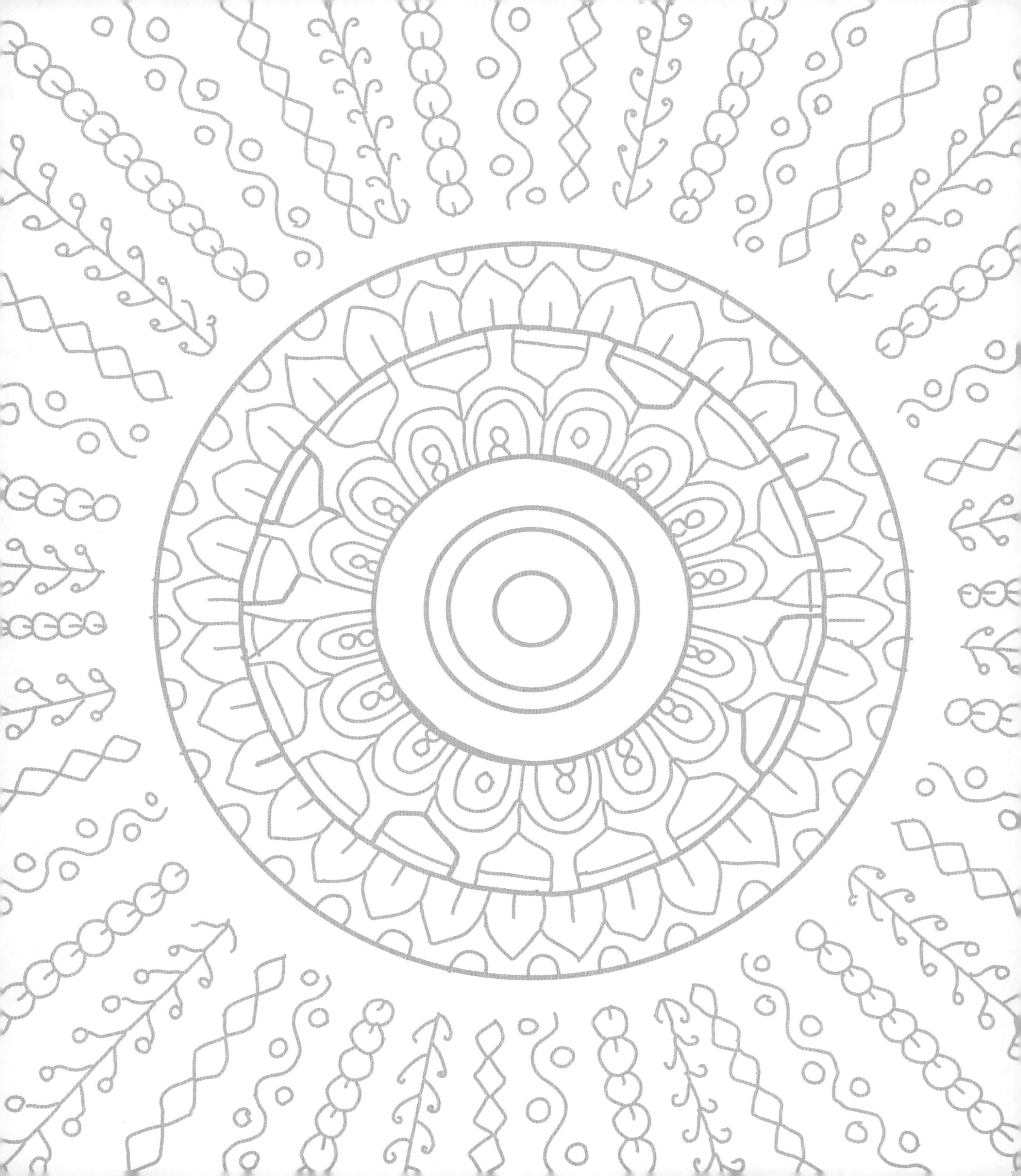

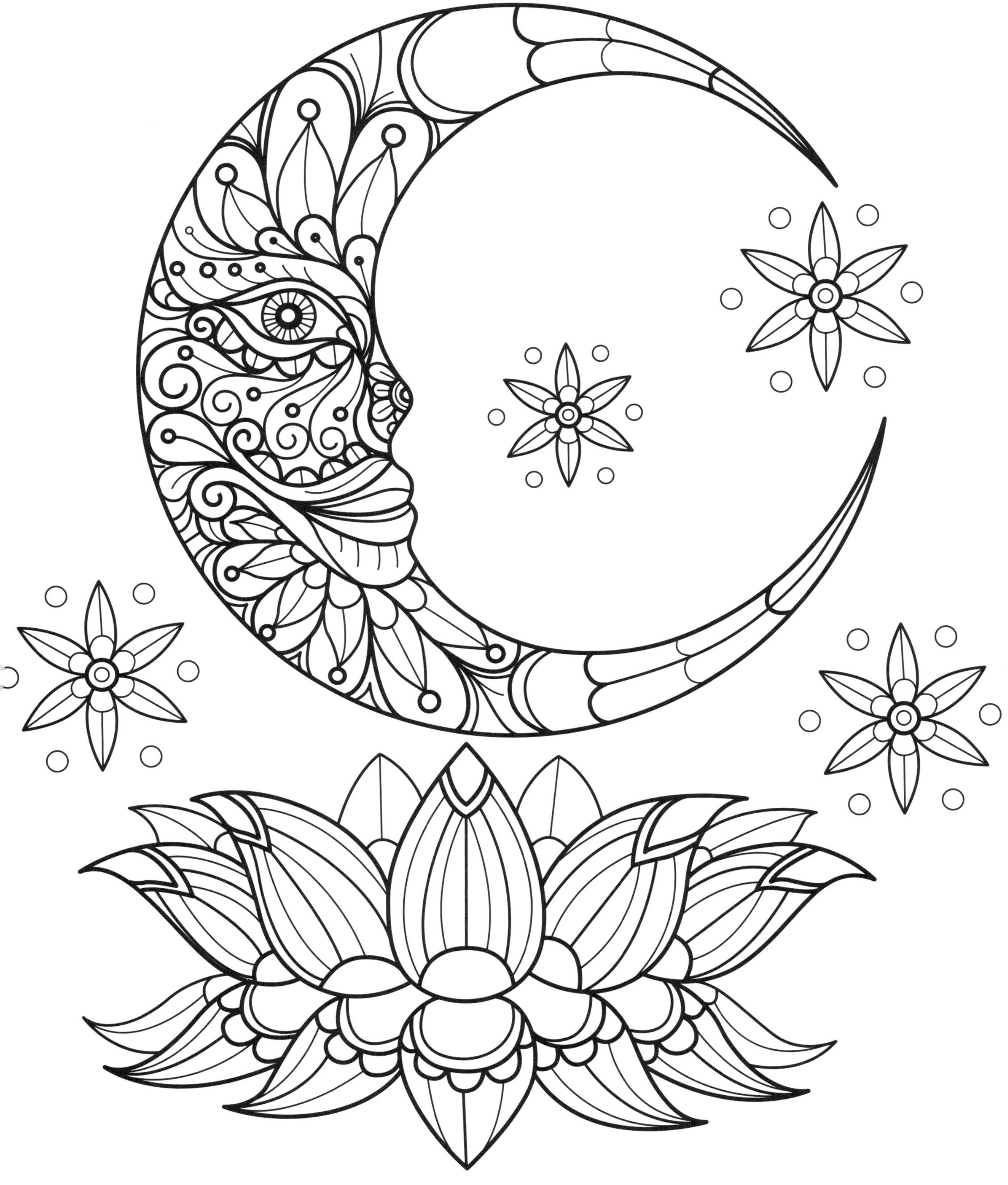

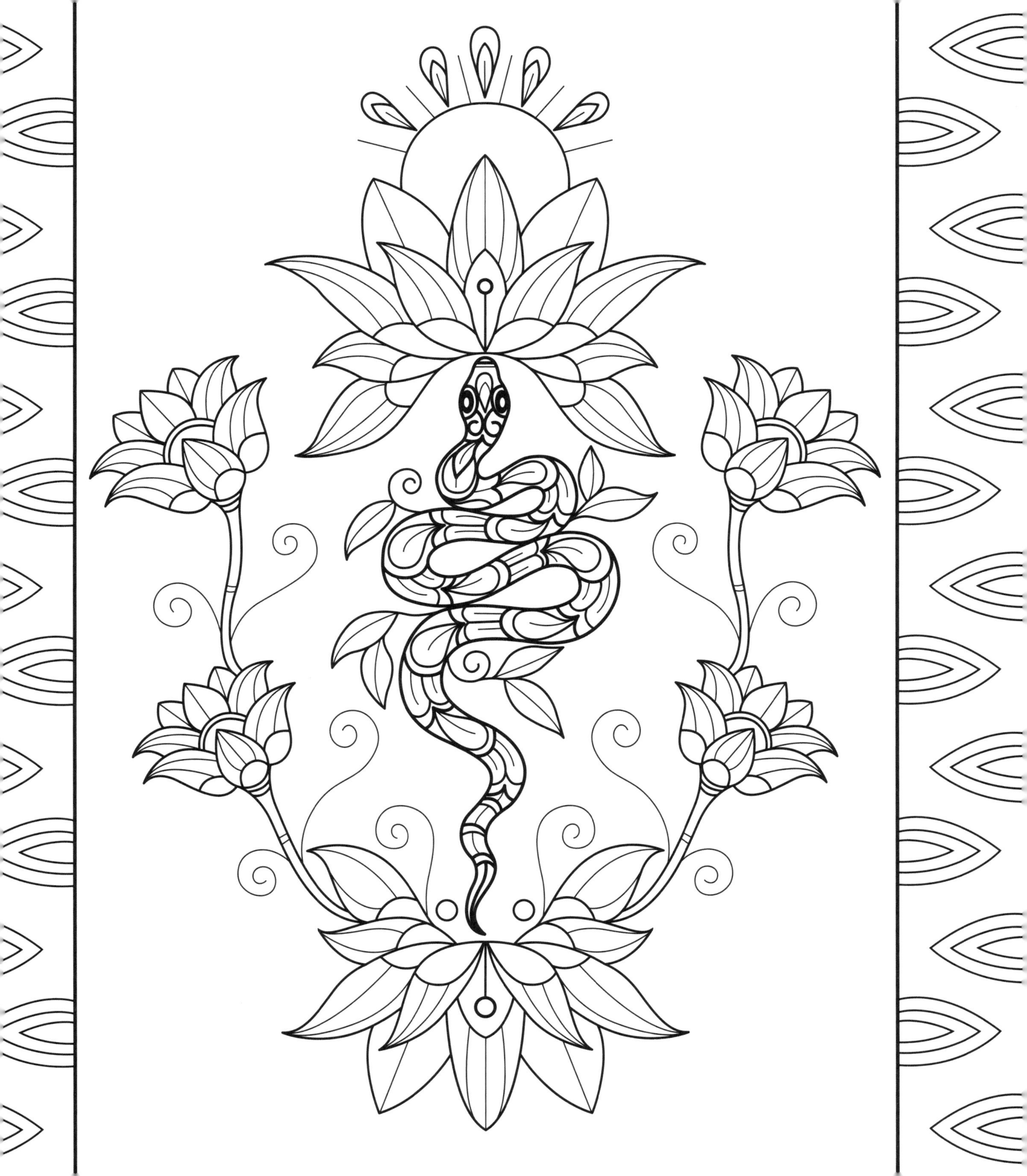

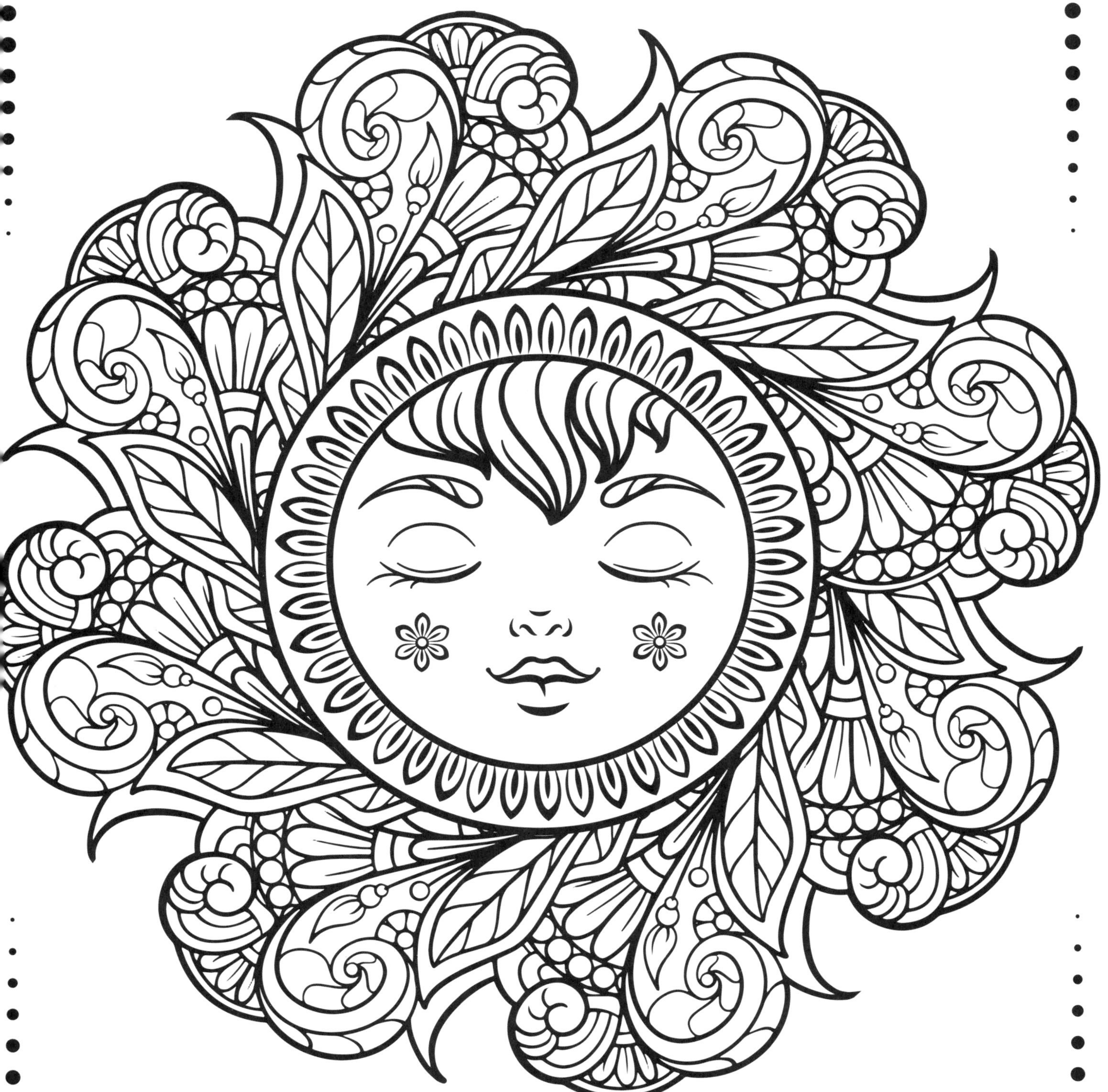

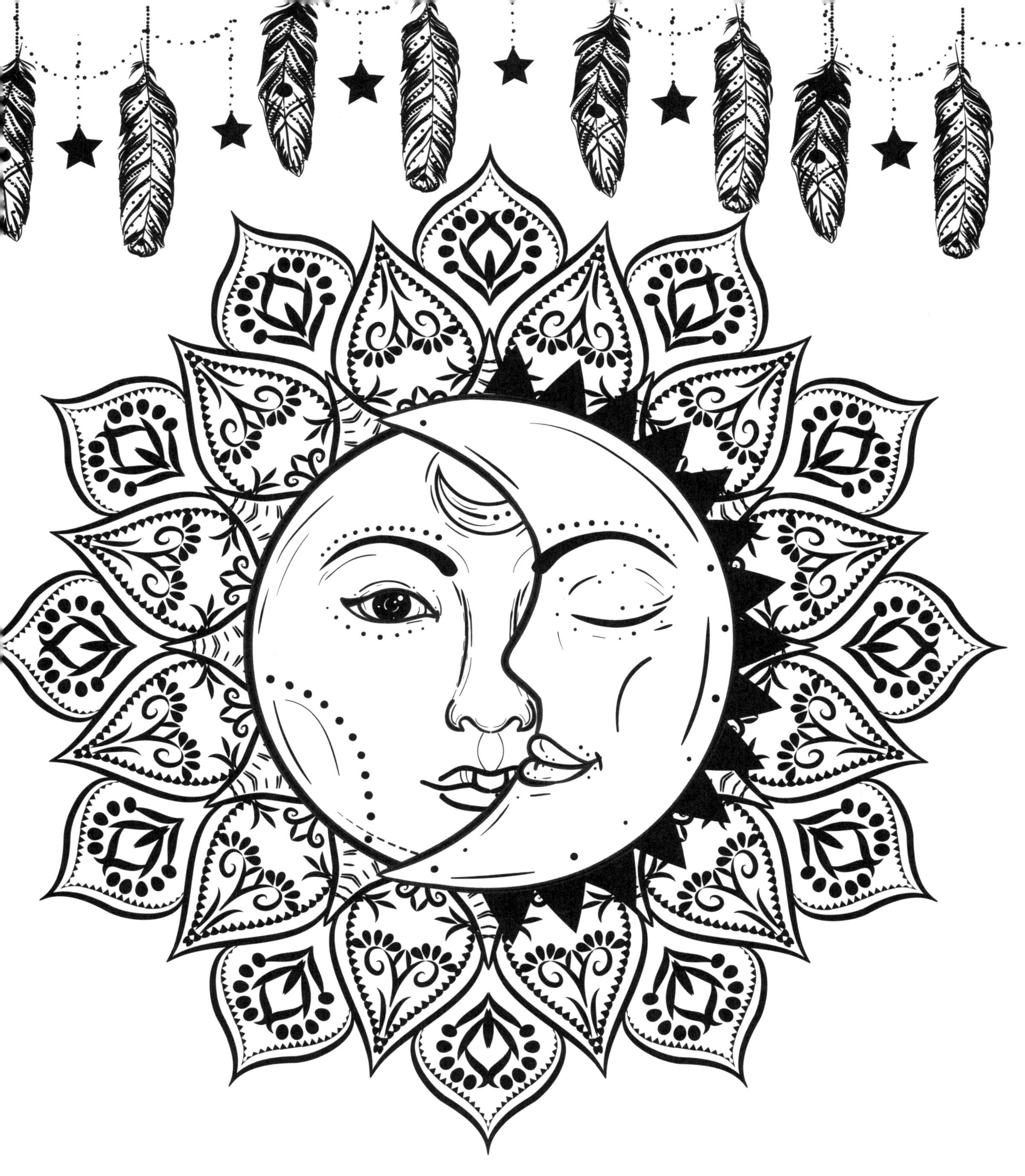